Why I Am a Charismatic

A Catholic Explains

*Reflections on
Charismatic Prayer
and the Longings
of the Human Heart*

Ronda Chervin, Ph.D.

Liguori Publications
One Liguori Drive
Liguori, MO 63057

Imprimi Potest:
Edmund T. Langton, C.SS.R.
Provincial, St. Louis Province
Redemptorist Fathers

Imprimatur:
St. Louis, June 15, 1978
+ John N. Wurm, S.T.D., Ph.D.
Vicar General, Archdiocese of St. Louis

ISBN 0-89243-089-3
Copyright © 1978, Liguori Publications
Printed in U.S.A.
Library of Congress Catalog Card Number: 78-62167

Cover design: Linda Harris

I would like to take this opportunity to express my special gratitude to:

Fr. Ralph Tichenor, S.J., for his discernment and wisdom;

the Loyola Marymount Renewal Community to which I belong, the prayer and witness of which are a constant inspiration and support;

and especially to Sister Francoise O'Hare, RSHM, for her fine editorial assistance.

The Fire and the Dove

In the lyrical imagery of the fire and the dove in Scripture, I find the key to the contemporary Catholic experience of prayer in the Spirit.

The Fire!

burning, purifying, enkindling
warmth and light!

Scripture proclaims:

I have come to cast fire upon the earth; and would that it were already kindled (Lk 12:49).

And there appeared to them tongues as of fire (Acts 2:3).

The Dove!

grace, gentle comfort, peace!

Scripture invites us:

Arise, my love, my fair one, and come away.
O my dove in the clefts of the rock (Song 2:13-14).

He will shelter thee under the shadow of his wings (Ps 36:8).

I saw the Spirit descend as a dove from heaven, and it remained on him . . . 'He on whom you see the Spirit descend and remain, this is he who baptizes with the Holy Spirit' (Jn 1:32-33).

Table of Contents

Charismatics expressing their joy in the Lord

Introduction:

A New
Pentecost

"Come, Holy Spirit, enkindle in us the fire of your love."

From within the holy Church of the 1960s, covered with the patina of centuries of sanctity and sin, a cry was rising: "Come, Holy Spirit." We hungered for the Church to show herself as a "light shining in the darkness." We longed to throw off the complacency of routine, that we might experience a deeper union with Christ, and serve as his leaven in the modern world.

The inspired deliberations of the bishops and the Holy Father which we find in the documents of Vatican II opened up innumerable new directions. But some interpretations of Vatican II also caused much confusion. Amidst a swirl of visible changes in the Church, the longings of the human heart for God, for certitude, for a firm hope in eternal life — these basic needs were submerged.

And then something as surprising as the lighting of a dove on the head of the Messiah spread like wildfire through the Church of the 1970s. It came both to sophisticated intellectuals and to unlettered rosary Catholics. It came to the middle-class parishes — to priests, to Brothers, and Sisters. Even bishops and cardinals felt the call.

This something even penetrated the screen separating Protestant sects; and new waves of conversion rose among the Lord's own people, the Jews. And this "something" that happened was not a "thing" at all, but a Person — the Third Person of the Blessed Trinity — coming to us!

What had been proclaimed throughout the centuries in each year's celebration of Pentecost was upon us — a totally new way to experience him!

The Approach of This Book

For the past eight years I have had the happiness of participating in this new experience of the Holy Spirit. As a woman who treasures the emotional side of religion, I am distressed at the way critics of charismatic prayer denigrate it as a cheap emotional high — a wave of enthusiasm destined to die the natural death of all fads.

Instead of trying to combat this attack by stressing the firm doctrinal foundations of the charismatic gifts, I would like to emphasize the way in which the release of the Holy Spirit within one meets the genuine longings of the human heart for absolute love, for faith, and for hope.

I shall begin by describing my own surprising encounter with the charismatic gifts of the Spirit several years ago. And then I will show why I think God wants to heal those of us who need healing from false resignation, lack of love, chronic doubt, and the miseries of despair.

Next I shall try to show how life in the Spirit leads to a new experience of the real presence of Christ in the sacraments, and to a fresh appreciation of Mary, our model, as the bride of the Spirit.

Finally, there will be a section giving responses to commonly heard questions about charismatic prayer. This section will take the form of an interview with Fr. Ralph T. Tichenor,S.J., professor of theology and philosophy at Loyola Marymount University and President of Southern California Renewal Communities.

The Spirit makes his presence felt

1

How the Holy Spirit Came to Give Me New Life

It was the summer of 1969. I was living in San Juan Capistrano, a small mission town in California. Hoping that the temperate climate might improve my husband's worsening asthma condition, our family had moved there from New York City.

For me, it was a time of crisis. My husband's health had deteriorated so badly that he could no longer carry on his work as president of a world-wide book distribution company. Our five-year-old twin daughters were about to start kindergarten. I had planned not to work full time until my children were teen-agers, but under the circumstances I was very glad that my husband insisted I finish my doctorate in philosophy and take up a regular teaching job.

In September I was to begin commuting to Los Angeles, 67 miles away, to take up the position of assistant professor of philosophy at Loyola University. My husband was to spend six months at the National Jewish Hospital in Denver, Colorado — a last-ditch attempt at a cure.

Before my husband's trip to Denver and my own first full-time teaching job, my twin sister, Carla De Sola, a well-known liturgical dancer, came to visit us during the summer. Carla was bubbling over with the strange news that she had received the gift of tongues!

You can understand why I so easily dismissed her experience when I explained that I was and still am what might be called a very conservative Catholic. A convert to the Catholic faith from a Jewish though atheistic background, I cling with tremendous fervor to the Church which is to me a light shining in the darkness.

At that time I particularly loved my daily Latin Mass. Each day I prayed the rosary for the conversion of my husband, practiced special devotions to the saints, and used all the intellectual power at my command to defend the doctrines of Catholicism against all doubters within and without the Church. I had an excellent spiritual guide to whom I submitted theological problems which arose, and I was totally averse to anything innovative unless it had been approved officially by Rome. With this in mind, you can imagine with what enthusiasm I greeted the announcement of my convert-sister that she was involved in a crazy new movement in the Church which claimed the gift of glossolalia (speaking in tongues)!

My sister's visit was to last most of the summer, spanning her teaching assignment at St. Joseph's College of Orange. So I decided not to pounce on her immediately with refutations of the gift of tongues. I decided to read up on the subject and marshal the best possible arguments. But materials about the movement were almost nonexistent, and my sister, a very peaceful and charming person, did not argue with me or try to push her new spirituality on me. So I tried to push the subject into the back of my mind. I love my sister dearly and I was eager to avoid an open confrontation.

However, very gently Carla would ask me one question which became a real annoyance: "Ronda, how do you express your closeness to the Holy Spirit?"

In spite of glaring faults, I regarded myself as an exemplary Catholic. But I had to confess that, to me, the Holy Spirit was more of a concept than a living Person. I also had difficulty believing that praying in tongues could go on in our times. I was of the opinion that the gift of tongues, a gift once given to the apostles for conveying the Gospel to people from many countries, was now defunct.

This background will help to explain why I could never regard the experience which was soon to follow as a natural result of my sister's influence or of mass psychology.

One evening after the children were in bed, and my husband had left for the clinic in Denver, I was alone with my sister. We were listening to a favorite piece of music on my husband's superb stereo equipment. The piece was the Bach B Minor Mass with its sublime crescendo of brass instruments proclaiming the "cum Sancto Spiritu" of the Gloria. I had always delighted in this particular movement. But I had never fully understood why a composer would select the coming of the Holy Spirit, to me a mere concept, for such ecstatic treatment.

At the peak of the victorious trumpet blasts when the singers intoned "cum Sancto Spiritu," I looked at my sister. To my amazement, her face had become transformed, as it were, into the face of Jesus! Unknown to herself it seemed as if the humble, merciful, loving countenance of Christ, as depicted by such artists as Rembrandt and El Greco, shone through her normal features. Drawn into the aura of this totally unexpected vision I said without any forethought: "Whatever you want to do to me about the Holy Spirit, go ahead!"

Surprised and somewhat dismayed — for she had little experience of the laying on of hands — Carla did place her hands on my head and prayed very, very softly. A tremendous flood of love and strength and happiness enveloped me and then some syllables in a strange language started coming into my mind. By then, it was rather late and I went to bed in a sort of daze.

When I awoke, I practically leaped out of bed for joy and all day long I felt on fire with love of God. The fire of the Spirit filled me with a soft, subtle, abiding sense of the dovelike presence of God within me. This quiet indwelling of the Spirit was something I had known before, but only as a fleeting grace. The great truths of the faith which I had always believed now seemed illumined and blazing with power. I could hardly wait to proclaim them afresh — not as intellectual doctrines, but as burning realities.

Ever since my sister prayed over me that night for the release of the Spirit, the quiet sense of God's loving presence has been with me.

Effects of the Spirit in My Life

There were very few charismatic prayer groups at that period. But even if I had found one nearby, I doubt, because of family responsibilities, that I would have participated. Several years went by during which I experienced the gifts of the Spirit privately rather than as part of a community.

The effects of the release of the Spirit on my life were profound. Once my university classes began, my program for weekdays included the inspiring early morning Mass at the Mission. After Mass I would drop off my girls at school, and then drive for an hour and a half to Los Angeles. During the trip I would praise God with great joy and pray for each of my students and for my teaching ministry.

At Loyola University I taught my classes in Christian philosophy with more than the usual fervor of a new teacher; for above all else, I was filled with the tremendous enthusiasm for truth which the Spirit brings.

In my zeal for the conversion of the students I had them write journals to which I responded sometimes with 10 pages of commentary. With these commentaries, I hoped to interweave with the students' subjective insights the objective truths of the faith which they considered irrelevant.

Most of the students were either lukewarm Sunday Catholics who went to church out of habit and duty with little joy in the Lord, or else were completely alienated from the Church. I decided to organize a soapbox witness campaign in which priests and Sisters, lay faculty and students were invited to come to a podium on the lawn at lunchtime and proclaim their belief.

About this same time a small number of Catholic Pentecostal students started a prayer meeting at the university. I was sympathetic to them, but reluctant to take time from counseling students in my office or from my home responsibilities.

I must confess, too, that I had greater trust in my own gifts than in the particular form prayer meetings were taking at that time. It was one thing to be prayed over by my sister in my own living room, and quite another to see strangers grouped on the floor laying hands on each other's heads. At the same time, I had to admit that I was running out of steam trying to do everything myself without the help of other Christians.

With the birth of my third child in 1971, the need for some new source of strength was especially felt. I had suffered through several miscarriages prior to this marvelous birth of our little son, Charles. It was a great joy to have him with us, but it was also very fatiguing. Then, besides my normal housework and care of the twins, there was my work at the university with the student journals to be annotated at home each evening.

In addition to these problems, the atmosphere at the university was getting worse. It was the rule rather than the exception to learn of priests and Sisters leaving their religious communities. Many of the lay faculty were barely remaining in the Church, their attitudes too tepid to make any form of witness possible. There were many fine Jesuits and Sisters who supported what I was doing. But in terms of day-by-day communication I felt pretty much isolated in my fiery apostolate.

Contact with the Prayer Group

Then something began to happen which could not fail to draw me toward the charismatic prayer group. Some students in my classes had been living dissolute life styles with consequent suicidal despair. Some of these students, for whom I had been praying night and day, reported that they had begun going to the charismatic prayer meeting and finding the light!

At the same time, priests who were among the most trustworthy and stable began to get involved in the prayer group. I was especially impressed when Fr. Ralph Tichenor, S.J., of Loyola and Fr. Philip Verhaegen, Prior of the Benedictine monastery of St. Andrew's, Valyermo, became leaders.

And so, after two years of staying away from the prayer group, I finally decided to give it a try.

Many critics suppose that people who flock to such prayer meetings are those who would go to anything out of loneliness, or because they had nothing better to do. That is certainly not my experience. From the moment I entered the meeting room I was attracted by the spirit of the group. The atmosphere was one of tremendous warmth and friendliness. They sang songs full of joy and enthusiasm. I could hardly believe that this could be going on right in the midst of the university with its then pervasive climate of doubt and cynicism. Here were hundreds of people singing, with absolute conviction and delight, words of simple faith. No polemics! No arguments! Just rejoicing in the Lord.

It seemed to me as if I had been transported back to the early Church. Right up in front were the lame, the sick, persons in wheelchairs, so that everyone could see them and pray for them.

All kinds of people were gathered there together in the love of Christ — long-haired hippies hugging policemen; blue-jeaned girls in sweat shirts in animated conversation with immaculately made-up models; priests, Sisters, and Brothers who previously had seemed distant — all reaching out with love in their hearts to all kinds.

And I mean *all* kinds! Can you imagine a teen-age boy in a shiny black jacket feeling free enough to tell a Catholic group that prior to his conversion he had occupied his spare evenings stealing the cars of parishioners attending novenas! What an inspiration to see these same novena-Catholics at the prayer meeting embracing "the prodigal son" as their brother!

I recall a woman telling how she had interpreted the Scripture about loving one's enemies to mean that she should pray for the women her husband was running around with; how eventually she won back her husband and even brought some of the women to Christ!

What gratitude I shall always feel for those young leaders of the group when I first began to attend the meetings. Steve Croskey, a student born a Catholic, had strayed into the drug culture and then came out of it through the graces of the Holy Spirit. Gabriel Meyer, a convert to the Catholic Church, had been a novice at a Camaldolese monastery, but had decided that his vocation lay in working in the world with people. Afire with the Spirit, these young people needed no doctorates to convey the truth. By virtue of their own intense excitement about the Gospel, they ushered us into the dynamic flow of the working of the Holy Spirit in our lives.

Graces That Flowed
from the Prayer Meetings

Between songs and witnessing and Scripture readings, there was time for praying in tongues. Having concentrated on the teaching ministry, I had not developed this gift at all. But here in the midst of what I liked to call "the gypsy Church," the words on my tongue began to pour forth from the depth of my soul in the form of beautiful melodies.

I began to come regularly to the prayer meetings. It was an experience of great joy in the companionship of people who had even more faith than I. The freedom flowing from the release of the Spirit in praise lifted me out of my previous exhaustion and gave me new hope. Even at times in the teaching cycle when I was again feeling very tired or depressed, the group was an enormous help. There was no need to hide unhappy states of mind from the brothers and sisters whom I encountered at the meetings. I could go up to anyone, even a stranger, and tell that person how I felt. I would then be prayed over until I let the Spirit come in to lift the burden.

Those who are familiar with the atmosphere of charismatic prayer meetings come to take such compassion for granted. But think for a moment about the way we normally feel at professional meetings, or even at church services. Don't we usually think that we have to maintain a "good image" no matter what? I know that I do. How different it is in a prayer group. There I can show my wounds, knowing that the sole interest of others is to comfort and help, not to judge.

After many years of participation in charismatic groups, I have come to believe that there is a special reason why people who attend such meetings are so compassionate. I think that Christ, in his providence, picks out the weakest people to draw close to himself, just as he did when he walked on earth. He knows that we are so needy that we have no strength to conceal our poverty of body and spirit. I am happy to number myself among those who are hungry and thirsty for God, among those who cannot resist the embrace of his overwhelming, merciful love. Once secure in his presence, we shall be the ones who can reach out to newcomers, accustomed as they often are to hiding their wounds behind a mask of false pride. We will be enabled to help them see that their deep need for salvation is their greatest asset.

Later on in this book I shall be discussing the nature of the different charismatic gifts of the Spirit. For the moment, let me just mention that as I started to attend the prayer meetings regularly, those gifts began to grow. I found that sometimes I could tell what the words of a tongue meant (the gift of interpretation). Strong images would well up in my heart seemingly from the Spirit (the beginning of the gift of prophecy). Warmth would flow into my hands in response to the sick or needy; I would be moved to lay hands on them and pray for them (the gift of healing).

A Mass followed the prayer meetings at the university. For me, as a traditional Catholic, greater than any of the charismatic gifts was the joy of witnessing so many people adoring Christ in the Eucharist. Here, among the charismatics, were throngs of the faithful discerning the Lord in the consecrated Host. At the words, "This is my body; this is my blood," a deep hush would fall over the crowd, to be followed by a ground swell of praise and adoration! In such a gathering I could see my beloved holy Mother Church rising up from the dust and ashes of post-conciliar confusion, full of the fire and love which was the true legacy of the Council.

Further Involvement and Spiritual Blessings

Pretty soon I was being asked to give talks to charismatic groups. What a different experience this was from teaching my cherished but lukewarm, doubting students! Instead of a group of people ready to "turn off" the minute God was mentioned, those who came to charismatic conferences and luncheons were hungry for God. They prayed fervently before, during, and after the talk. They welcomed God's truth from the mouth of the speaker, and expected his living presence to be among them.

If you have ever had to give any kind of speech, even a little one, you will know how nervous one can get just before beginning. How comforting it is, then, to be surrounded by a warm greeting committee who will take the speaker aside and pray for her. Freedom from the artificial barriers of convention, which characterizes people in this movement, will always be to me one of the most cherished gifts of the Spirit.

About this time I had the privilege of being asked to be part of the team of a *Life in the Spirit* seminar for students. The seminar is a sequence of talks, discussion, and group prayer, designed to prepare newcomers to receive the release of the Spirit's gifts. I remember one young woman who came to the seminar looking like a typical, popular party girl. At the climax of the meetings when we laid hands on her head and prayed for her, she radiated with purity of heart.

Another participant was a religious Brother who had received the gifts of the Spirit previously but had experienced difficulty manifesting them openly. What an honor it was for me as a lay person to participate in the work of the Spirit in this young man!

We have no right to invade the privacy of others in their relationship to God. Yet in the Mystical Body, when the privilege is given, the fruits can be very great for both people involved.

Naturally, the great moments of infusion of grace do not necessarily sanctify a person's whole life. For some, no doubt, the moment passes and life goes on as usual. But as I have followed the progress of young people who have gone on in a firm commitment to the Spirit, I have witnessed quite remarkable spiritual strength. With social life at the university, I find it a sure sign of God's blessing when students adopt a life style which includes practices such as Mass each day and an hour of prayer; regular times of fellowship and counsel; witnessing through CCD teaching and giving retreats and conferences; and service to the poor in the community.

The new fire of the Spirit enkindled prayer meetings, and the dovelike comforting of my Christian brothers and sisters gave me strength to initiate another phase of ministry. Through the journals kept by my students, I had become very conscious of the difficulties they encounter each day. I hoped to reach them by writing books designed specially to meet their needs.

My first book, *Church of Love,* published by Liguori Publications, is based on the analogy between Christ's love for us and the romantic love which human beings experience for one another. Should not the love of the Savior be as self-giving, intimate, and transforming as the encounter of love between men and women? Is not the Son the *self*-giving of the Father? Are not the sacraments his way of reaching deep into our very being? And are not the many-faceted gifts of truth, example, and community within the Church the source of our transformation?

In spite of the demands of household life with young children milling around, I was able, through the power of the Spirit's teaching gifts, to write another book, *The Art of Choosing,* also published by Liguori Publications.

The Spirit in Family and Private Life

Speaking of the home, I should mention a very significant phase in my life as a charismatic which began at a regional conference. Several of the women present realized that our respective family lives were not as renewed in the Spirit as

God wished. Many of us had great joy in the Lord at prayer meetings, which spilled over into the readiness to be better wives and mothers. By the middle of the week, however, we would find ourselves out of steam and at the mercy of irritability, resentment, or anxiety. From the frank sharing of our weaknesses came the inspiration to meet together once a week in the morning for a mothers' prayer group.

The year I was involved in leading the mothers' group was a turning point in my family relationships. Through sharings, prayer, and Scripture study about common problems of marriage and parenthood, we began to develop new ways of relating to those repetitive, tension-filled situations in our family lives. The truths I felt the Spirit taught us during this time I subsequently wrote up as a series of booklets: *Prayer and Your Everyday Life, The Spirit and Your Everyday Life,* and *Love and Your Everyday Life,* published also by Liguori Publications.

By no means did we solve all of our family problems that year at mothers' group meetings. We still constantly find ourselves falling back into worldly patterns of dealing with things. But there is one big difference: we have hope. When I meet any Christian mother in the playground, instead of trying to put up a fake image of being a perfect wife or mother — or, worse still, just complaining together and building up our right to be resentful — we can speak openly and pray about our problems. We have been led out of our cave of isolated, brooding self-pity into the light of the Spirit.

In my own life, I know I can count on the prayerful concern of people in the community of the Spirit. For example, when my husband is especially ill I can call on people and know that they will give much more than perfunctory attention to the need. In some cases households of young charismatics will practice fasting for the intention of a healing. At this point my husband, though not without some symptoms, is much better and able to work.

The call of the Spirit is not only to outward acts and ministries. It is also an invitation to deep, quiet prayer. Once a person is opened to the living presence of Christ through the release of the Spirit, prayer becomes a response to a constant call to be with our divine Lover. There is a wordless inclination to pray and praise at every time and place — on the freeway, in the chapel, in the shower, in the middle of the night, when we embrace the beloved members of our families.

We know that Christ is with us, waiting for us to lift up to him our compulsive preoccupations and worries, waiting for us to sit at his feet as did the Magdalene. He is always present; we have but to turn inward to him.

What you have read so far may lead you to consider involvement — or deeper involvement — in charismatic prayer. But you may still have doubts. "Yes," you may say, "it sounds good, but So-and-So who are charismatics appear so phony to me." We will come to this and other questions later in this book. But first, I would like to delve still more deeply into the well of feelings — into the common emotions of loneliness, anger, temptation, doubt, and despair. We all experience these feelings as we struggle with the crosses of life, and I believe it is in these areas that charismatic prayer has very much to offer. We need to open the hidden pain of our lives to the healing comfort of the Lord within his Mystical Body. If we are to follow his commandment to spread faith, hope, and love in the world, we desperately need to experience his love more and more deeply within ourselves and in our daily living.

Experiencing deep peace in the Spirit

(2)

Beyond
Resignation

There is a certain attitude that could be summarized in the following terms:

"Love is not primarily an emotion; it is a decision to act lovingly. You should not be alarmed if you find that there is very little felt love in your heart. The feeling of love is only an initial, immature phase of Christian love; the real thing is service.

"As for doubts about religious truths, doubt is compatible with faith. For it is of the essence of faith to be unsure, to grope in the dark. God is a mystery. You should accept doubts as part of the process of life.

"It is too idealistic to expect always to be filled with hope, for there are dark periods of despair in every life. What is necessary is to do your best no matter what you feel. Don't worry about seeing good results. Maybe there is life after death and maybe there isn't. Meanwhile, it is good to immerse yourself in life and let its currents buoy you up and let you down, without trying to put a pious meaning on everything."

The frame of mind described above can be called *resignation*. On the plane of human relationships we can recognize it very clearly in marriages where each partner does his or her duty with little sense of love, a great deal of hidden doubt about the wisdom of the marriage in the first place, and almost no hope for mutual joy.

An Answer to Resignation

Some practicing Catholics whose attitudes toward God have become loveless, permeated by doubt, and with very little hope of renewal, find the atmosphere of charismatic prayer meetings positively "unreal."

Some people say: "Many of these charismatics appear to be nowhere near as 'authentic,' 'self-sacrificing,' or 'searching' as some people outside their circle. So how could they be experiencing such closeness to God? What they are experiencing must be a result of group psychology. These charismatics must be emotionally unbalanced. Even if they are sincere in their longings, their answers are much too simplistic. Only saints have such supernatural experiences — and these people certainly are not saints."

After years of thought about such challenges to charismatic prayer, I have come to this conclusion: Resignation to doubt, to despair, and to the absence of felt love is a terrible sickness in the Church. It is not to be justified as authentic, but to be healed by the Holy Spirit.

The examples of love we see in Scripture are always warm and personal. Jesus compares his love to that of a mother hen with her chicks (Mt 23:37). The love of the Father is so overpowering that he rushes toward us anticipating our return as in the image of the Prodigal Son (Lk 15). In response to the great love God has for us, we are enjoined to heartfelt trust. When David of the Psalms or when Jesus himself underwent deep suffering, their attitude was never one of resignation. Rather, they cried out in pain until God reassured them.

We see in Scripture that the examples of faith are not of resignation to doubt. Job doubts. Thomas doubts. But they do not remain in doubt. They challenge God until they see the light.

Can you imagine that a child who doubted who his real father was would simply resign himself to being unsure? Such a son would have to have a very ambiguous relationship to the man whose fatherhood he doubted to resign himself to ignorance about the bond between them.

As the English writer C. S. Lewis points out in *Pilgrim's Regress,* most of us do have a somewhat ambiguous attitude toward God, the Father. Part of us would like to be free to follow our own wishes with no one to judge us. Part of us prefer to doubt the existence of God rather than to have a firm faith that calls for perfect obedience.

We see in Scripture that hope is a leap of trust in God's power, regardless of all human reasons for despair. God is depicted as mighty, able to do anything, wanting us to place all our hope in him.

Can you imagine Moses praying, "God, I know that you want us just to help ourselves without any intervention from you. So we are going to carve a path patiently through the waters of the Red Sea so you can see how powerful we are."

Can you imagine Jesus praying, "God, I have no idea if resurrection is possible, but I'm going to try my hardest to conquer death." "Lazarus, come forth!"

True, there are times when we must accept the answer "No" to some cherished wish. But our abandonment to God's providence includes the faith that he *could* do it; that placing our trust in him is no childish hope in Santa Claus, but the conviction that God is intimately involved in every life he sustains.

The importance of going *beyond* resignation in our longings for love, faith, and hope will become even clearer as we first describe several states of mind on the human level, and then describe these same states as they are experienced in the Holy Spirit.

The Fire of Love

To feel unlovable . . .
what is that really like?

I look in the mirror and I see my face: ugly, blotchy, ill-shapen, lined, puffy, drab, pouty . . .
   eyes — bleary, heavy, pathetically, stupidly yearning . . . for what?
   body — too short, too tall, too fat, too thin, too weak, too bulging . . . .

I look into my soul and it looks ugly . . . full of fruitless schemes, petty resentments, despicable self-pity.

What do strangers think of me? I know. They think I'm stupid, phony, ridiculous, arrogant, envious, mean, silly, conceited, pushy, mediocre.

What do my family and friends think of me? They think I'm obnoxious, contemptible, irritating, dumb, unchangeable, domineering, demanding, a weight around their necks from which they cannot escape because our lives are interwoven and we need one another to survive.

I lug this ugly and hateful self to church each week. As I sit in my pew, I look around and reassure myself that everyone else is as unlovable as I.

If I happen to see someone who looks a cut above the rest, then each week I scrutinize that person carefully, searching for flaws. And when I have found them, I smile complacently and resume my comfortable mumbling of the well-known prayers.

And when I feel so unlovable, I am ready to sell myself for any tiny bit of consolation;

my integrity for a moment's pleasure in getting advantage over an enemy:

my dignity for a moment's pleasure in an extra amount of unneeded food or drink;

my purity for a moment's pleasure in the oblivion of a sexual thrill.

Feeling unlovable — what a potent cause of sin!

To feel lovable . . .
what is that really like?

I look in the mirror and I see the funny, amazing reality of my own face, my spirit shining through all the patently obvious defects.

I rejoice at having hair and eyes and nose and mouth; satisfied to be a person.

I look at my body — the tremendous, mysterious gift which enables me to live on earth. Fat, thin, short, tall — how accidental these outer appearances are, compared to the sheer miracle of being alive.

I look into my soul and smile, "You are beautiful, my heart, because you yearn for goodness even in the midst of the human muddle of your life, most of which is of your own making!"

What do strangers think of me? Well, it doesn't matter, does it? Instead of looking at them looking at me, I just look at them and marvel at their variety. How lovable they are, in spite of themselves!

What do my family and friends think of me? How they must love me to put up with all my unpleasant qualities so well known to them, my faithful victims!

I bring my strange, dear, unique self to church and enjoy solidarity with all those other unique people who persevere no matter what, because they hope in God.

To feel loved in the Spirit . . .
what is that really like?

To close my eyes to all human mirrors and let the fire of God's love descend, burning through the layers of ugliness and self-hatred . . . burning right into the depth of my being, there to respark the original flame of the divine which was my baptismal gift.

"I have called you by name: you are mine. When you pass through the water, I will be with you . . . . For I am the Lord your God, the Holy One of Israel, your savior" (Is 43:1-3). This beautiful passage, which my godfather wrote out for me to meditate on, gives me a sense of being loved for myself in the Spirit.

Healed in the purifying fire of the Spirit, I see the inner face of my own absolutely unique spirit. He fashioned the inmost core of me which is made in the beauty of his image.

I hear the special mystic melody of his love song . . . the haunting music of some tongue deeper than my own consciousness . . . a melody conducted by the Spirit in the lover's trysting place of my wounded heart.

Drawn by the Spirit into the wounded heart of the Savior, I am comforted, and sin loses all its taunting glamour. This greater love casts lower loves from the pedestal of idol-worship.

In the light of the Spirit I glimpse what God sees when he looks at his beloved family of man:

Like a lover I see the graceful deerlike spirit of another person flash by and hide behind the trees of ordinary contact, to be drawn out only by Christian love.

Like a mother I press to myself the frightened little child hidden inside every adult . . . I offer food and shelter to the needy . . . spending my life in their service.

Like a father discerning a need, I place a warm, protecting arm around another . . . beating down the mighty walls of injustice.

Like brothers and sisters in happy times, we rejoice in the celebration of life, in the praise of the Lord, valuing all persons no matter how sinful, forgiving, washing their feet, serving them, especially those entrusted to us.

Are these depthless feelings into which the Holy Spirit leads us to be dismissed as hypocrisy simply because, in daily living, we fail over and over again to do them justice? Should we flee from light and warmth because we are still so dark and cold-hearted? Should we not rather return constantly to the burning heart of the Savior, present to us within the community which is his Body, and proclaim with St. Paul:

"For I am sure that neither death, nor life, nor angels, nor principalities, nor things present, nor things to come, nor powers, nor height, nor depth, nor anything else in all creation, will be able to separate us from the love of God in Christ Jesus our Lord" (Rom 8:38-39).

The Fire of Faith

What does it feel like to doubt?

I wake up in the night and I think: "Each of these men and women thinks that he or she is a little hunk of matter destined to be buried under five feet of dirt, and that's it?"

I go to Mass and I think: "Suppose all of this is just mumbo jumbo, a crust of superstition we have believed for so long that we keep coming even though there is nothing to it — like the story of the emperor's new clothes. After all, we're not children who believe in magic. Who can really imagine that bread and wine become God? That's ridiculous — or is it? I don't know, so why do I come?"

I think of the laws of the Church and think: "How rigid and archaic. Why should people suffer and suffer when science has such good solutions to the muddles we get into. Should a person pay all her life for the sin of forgetting to take a birth control pill, or for marrying the wrong person in the glow of the first experience of sex?"

Probably there is a God. After all, something doesn't come out of nothing. But who knows what he is really like? What kind of God lets people die agonizing deaths from cancer? What kind of God watches in superior detachment while millions of innocent Jews are gassed in concentration camps, or Christians are tortured in Communist prisons?

Maybe there is no way to know. Maybe we must be satisfied to muddle along, trying to do the best we can and hope that life turns out to be better than it seems.

What is human faith like?

I wake up in the night and I hear my husband breathing quietly beside me. I rise and peek into the rooms of the children, all snug and cozy under their comforters. All is well.

Who can doubt the goodness of life when there is so much of it in every square inch of reality — if only we will look. I ride on the subway to work. I look at all those careworn but good, faithful faces. What keeps these people going day after day to jobs which cannot be very gratifying? It must be love of their families. Or, if they are single, it must be a basic faith in life as worthwhile, a faith that the joys outweigh the pain. It is good to be alive.

I go to church and I am happy to see people together expressing their faith in life and in each other. It doesn't matter to me any more whether the rites of the Mass are symbols or gates through which the Sacred Presence comes. God is love and love is God. Whatever displays the drama of human love, its self-offering, its crucifixion, its rising to new life . . . is good.

The laws of the Church? Most of them are pretty sound ethics . . . and when it comes to the controversial ones, let people put faith in their own consciences. God gave us minds, which he wants us to use.

What is the infused faith of the Holy Spirit like?

I wake up in the night, gripped by dread fear and doubt. Then the Spirit prompts me to reach out in the darkness toward the light of Christ. Slowly his holy presence surrounds me, and in that light I visualize all of humankind sleeping in the palm of God's hand.

I rise early and, though half asleep, begin to let the Spirit pray in me, "Behold the handmaid of the Lord, be it done to me according to your word." After the morning wake-up routine, I open the Scriptures and let the Spirit breathe his truth where he will, sending me the message for my day. "Did not our hearts burn within us, while he talked to us on the road, while he opened to us the Scriptures?" (Lk 24:32)

I get into my car and drive to work. On the way, hymns come to my life and I praise God in song. Arriving at my job I silently pray for all those with whom I work, knowing that they are but slightly disguised citizens of the eternal kingdom. I offer the drudgery and fatigue of my work for my family and for my fellow workers. I ask the Spirit to help me to see the day in terms of his truth that I may not slip into competitiveness, bickering, gossip, envy, and other unchristian ways.

I go to holy Mass, the summit of each day or of every week. There is the pure, unadulterated presence of my Lord himself, speaking in the words of Scripture. I pray for openness to what the priest will say in his homily. Even when I am distracted, I feel happy to stand and recite the Creed, that great summation of the love story of God for man. I truly believe that the Lord is my Savior and so I let the Spirit lift my heart in praise as I watch the great sacrifice of Christ being reenacted on the altar. I am happy to express my unity with the other believers as the Spirit fills the sign of peace with holy love. I acknowledge my unworthiness, but come eagerly to the altar to receive my Lord and my God who loves me so much that he wishes to enter and dwell within me.

The Mass is over. The fire of faith infused in me by the Holy Spirit makes me long to witness to him all through the day or the week. If only I could follow the delicate leadings of the Spirit, never substituting the lies of the Evil One, but placing all my confidence in God's truth.

I trust in his Word and his sacrifice for me, and so I do not allow discouragement with my own failures to make me doubt his love and his plan for me.

When I read articles or books which call into question the truths of the faith or the moral doctrines of the Church, I do not trust human reason as infallible. I have faith in the working of the Holy Spirit through the ministry of the bishops, with the Pope as the final authority in matters of dispute. With this faith, I turn to the writings which express infallible truth and read them prayerfully in the expectancy of discerning the truth more clearly.

On the Wings of the Dove of Hope

What does it feel like to despair?

I try and try and try, and it makes no difference. I will never succeed, because life is a cheat. Even well-intentioned people are too selfish to live happily together. There is always conflict, never harmony. I am probably my own worst enemy.

I feel so frustrated. No one follows my good advice, and then I have to watch them sink into the quicksand of their stupid choices. I see my loved ones getting deeper and deeper into trouble, and I cannot rescue them because they flee from my guidance.

My life is empty. I have everything I ever dreamed of — a beautiful house, a new car each year, a boat, a cabin. But it makes so little difference. I have to drink myself into a stupor to get through the evening.

I am sick and useless. Each day I awaken to a nightmare of pain, disability, diminishment of my powers. Of what value is my life, now that I am a burden to all who love me? Soon they will cast me aside and abandon me to strangers.

What do I have to live for? Death alone will welcome me.

Hope is a mirage in the desert. We have to hope to keep on living, but there is nothing to hope for. The darkness grows darker, and the light grows dimmer.

What is human hope like?

No matter how many times I fail, I always pick myself up and try again. I care too much just to watch things deteriorate and not do anything about them. Sometimes even failure can lead to a better creative solution.

I have hope even when I don't see results right away. I believe that every well-intentioned act has to bear fruit eventually. Sometimes people I love go off the deep end, but I am sure that they will come back on the right track.

Though the world situation is terrible, there are little acts of individuals which bring hope. Even in concentration camps where despair seemed to be the only logical attitude, there were people who helped others and thereby saved themselves. If each person reaches out in hope at the worst times, surely the suffering in the world will diminish.

What is hope in the Spirit like?

As I read the Scriptures, the Holy Spirit brings me the infinite comfort of the truth: the Father's love, climaxed in the giving of his Son for men. I watch Jesus bringing hope to the crippled, the sick, the greedy, and the Magdalenes. I see his merciful love conquering their shame and dread, and stripping away the prideful bravado which rationalizes sin.

"Come to me all who labor and are heavy laden, and I will give you rest" (Mt 11:28). "O Jerusalem, Jerusalem . . . how often would I have gathered your children together as a hen gathers her brood under her wings, and you would not!" (Lk 13:34)

How much of our despair comes from a wrong image of the Father, conceived (often in the image of our own fathers) as fierce or disappointing or as an unpredictable teaser who can never be figured out or placated.

And when we fail to hope in God as a loving Father, then we give in to the temptation of placing too much hope in ourselves or in other human beings to bring about the good as we see it. We scheme and push to get our own way; we manipulate others by flattery or bribes. And finally, we end by trying to control even God himself through prayer-bargaining. "If I pray more often, or to yet another saint, then you will have to come through with what I want, God!"

How different it is to rely wholly on the Spirit. When I look at Jesus in the Gospels, I don't see him plotting to save the world. He does just the opposite. During the temptations in the desert he rejects all the power-grabbing schemes which Satan suggests. He humbly approaches John the Baptist, who is not at all his equal, in order to be anointed by the Spirit. The Dove, the Holy Spirit, descends, and immediately the disciples and those in need of healing come to recognize who Jesus is: the One in whom they should place their own personal salvation and the hope of Israel.

So should we, contemporary followers of Jesus, learn to hope. Humbly we should seek the anointing of the Spirit given at the hands of those we perhaps deem to be less than ourselves. Then, placing all hope in the Spirit we shall be healed of the temptation to despair of our Father's love. Gradually the time and energy we previously put into a vain attempt to save ourselves will be released into ministry for others. For if we have trust that God is taking care of us, then we can spare the time to place others first.

When we tend to fall back into self-hatred, doubt, and despair, when we struggle with our roles as fathers and mothers, students, workers, and consecrated religious, let us bow our heads for a fresh anointing. "Be still and know that I am God" (Ps 46:11).

"As the Word of the Lord raised Lazarus from the dead, may the fiery wind of the Holy Spirit unwind the funeral clothes of our resignation, that our true selves may come forth reborn in his presence for the spreading of the Kingdom of Love on earth as it is in heaven."

Pope Paul VI speaks to charismatics (1975)

3

The Charismatic Gifts of the Spirit and the Renewal of the Church

Is it really Catholic to seek the charismatic gifts of the Spirit?

There are many who associate speaking in tongues, prophecy, and healing with the Pentecostal Churches. And so, in their minds, there is a contradiction between such manifestations and Catholicism. I hope that the final section of this book, which consists of an interview with a priest-leader of the charismatic renewal, will answer such questions on a doctrinal level. What I will try to do in this chapter, from the standpoint of a lay participant, is to show why these charismatic gifts are so important for the Church with its present-day problems.

In order to understand the mission of the Holy Spirit in Catholic life today, it is important to distinguish two aspects of the reality of the Church:

(1) The first aspect is the *holiness* of the Church — all the grace, wisdom, prayer, love, mercy, and sacrifice present in our midst as we journey to eternity.

(2) The second aspect is the *sinfulness* in the Church — all the betrayal, worldliness, self-righteousness, legalism, and cynical indifference.

Every generation of Catholics participates in both these aspects of the Church. At each moment we are either perpetuating sinfulness in the Church by our compromise with evil and injustice, or we are strengthening the forces of renewal.

The history of the Church reveals a cycle of fervor, decline, internal reform movements, splits, new fervor, decline. . . . A time of decline may be likened to dust and ashes. We cannot set the dead ashes afire with mere human good will. What we need is the supernatural fire of the Holy Spirit.

The workings of the Holy Spirit always come as a surprise. For example, who would have guessed that the remedy for the decadent Church of the early Middle Ages would be a radical embracing of total poverty by one rich young man — St. Francis!

And isn't it just as unbelievable that the Spirit would rekindle faith among complacent, worldly Catholics of the early 20th century by means of apparitions of the Holy Virgin to poor illiterate children?

And once again, it was far from the minds of those praying for Church renewal during Vatican II that the Holy Spirit would come to thousands of Catholics in the form of the charismatic gifts of the Spirit.

(Anyone who wishes to trace the amazing spread of the charismatic movement in today's Church should read the book *Catholic Pentecostals,* by Kevin and Dorothy Ranaghan [Paulist Press, 1969]. A more recent work explaining the charismatic renewal theologically, by well-known Catholic theologian René Laurentin, is *Catholic Pentecostalism* [Doubleday, 1977].)

In May of 1975, Pope Paul VI gave a lengthy address to an international conference of charismatics in Rome. The Pope's address indicates clearly where the dangers lie if the experience of the Holy Spirit in charismatic prayer is isolated from the Spirit's other gifts to the Church. But there is no suggestion in the

Holy Father's address that charismatic gifts are an invasion of the Church by practices of merely psychological origin.

The Address of Pope Paul VI

Pope Paul said:

"You have chosen the city of Rome in this Holy Year to celebrate your Third International Congress, dear sons and daughters. You have asked us to meet you today and to address you. You have wished thereby to show your attachment to the church founded by Jesus Christ and to everything that this See of Peter represents for you.

"This strong desire to situate yourselves in the church is an authentic sign of the action of the Holy Spirit. For God became man in Jesus Christ, of whom the church is the Mystical body; and it is in the church that the Spirit of Christ was communicated on the day of Pentecost when he came down upon the apostles gathered in the upper room, 'in continuous prayer,' with Mary, the mother of Jesus (cf. Acts 1:13-14).

". . . the church and the world need more than ever that 'the miracle of Pentecost should continue in history' . . . In fact, inebriated by his conquests, modern man has finished by imagining, according to the expression used by the last Council, that he is free 'to be an end unto himself, the sole artisan and creator of his own history' (Gaudium et Spes, 20). Alas! Among so many of those very people who continue by tradition to profess God's existence and through duty to render him worship, God has become a stranger in their lives!

"Nothing is more necessary to this more and more secularized world than the witness of this 'spiritual renewal' that we see the Holy Spirit evoking in the most diverse regions and milieux. The manifestations of this renewal are varied: a profound communion of souls, intimate contact with God, in fidelity to the commitments undertaken at Baptism, in prayer — frequently in group prayer — in which each person, expressing himself freely, aids, sustains and fosters the prayer of the others and, at the basis of everything, a personal conviction which does not have its source solely in a teaching received by faith, but also in a certain lived experience.

"This live experience shows that without God man can do nothing, that with him, on the other hand, everything becomes possible. Hence this need to praise God, thank him, celebrate the marvels that he works everywhere about us and within us.

"Human existence rediscovers its 'relationship to God,' what is called the 'vertical dimension,' without which man is irremediably crippled . . . .

"How then could this 'spiritual renewal' not be good fortune for the church and for the world? And how, in this case, could one not take all the means to ensure that it remains so?

"These means, dear sons and daughters, the Holy Spirit will certainly wish to show you himself, according to the wisdom of those whom the Holy Spirit himself has established as 'guardians, to feed the church of God' (Acts

20:28). For it is the Holy Spirit who inspired Saint Paul with certain very precise directives, directives that we shall content ourselves with recalling to you. To be faithful to them will be for you the best guarantee for the future.

Three Principles for Discernment

"You know the importance that the apostle attributed to the spiritual gifts. 'Never try to suppress the Spirit,' he wrote to the Thessalonians (1 Thes 5:19), while immediately adding: 'Test everything, hold fast what is good' (v. 21). Thus he considered that a discernment was always necessary, and he entrusted the task of testing to those whom he had placed over the community (cf. v. 12). With the Corinthians, a few years later, he enters into great detail. In particular, he indicates to them three principles in the light of which they will more easily be able to practice this indispensable discernment.

1. "The first principle by which he begins his exposé is fidelity to the authentic doctrine of the faith (1 Cor 12:1-3). Anything that contradicted it would not come from the Spirit.

"He who distributes his gifts is the same one who inspired the Scriptures and who assists the living magisterium of the church, to whom, according to the Catholic faith, Christ entrusted the authentic interpretation of these Scriptures. This is why you experience the need for an even deeper doctrinal formation: biblical, spiritual, theological. Only a formation such as this, whose authenticity must be guaranteed by the hierarchy, will preserve you for ever possible deviations and give you the certitude and joy of having served the cause of the Gospel without 'beating the air' (1 Cor 9:26).

2. "The second principle: all spiritual gifts are to be received with gratitude; and you know that the list is long (1 Cor 12:4-10; 28-30), and does not claim to be complete (cf. Rom 12:6-8; Eph 6:11).

"Given, nevertheless, 'for the common good' (1 Cor 12:7), they do not all procure this common good to the same degree. Thus the Corinthians are to 'desire the higher gifts' (v. 31), those most useful for the community (cf. 14:1-5).

3. "This third principle is the most important one in the thought of the apostle . . . . No matter how desirable spiritual goods are — and they are desirable — only the love of charity, *agape*, makes the Christian perfect; it alone makes people pleasing to God . . . .

"This love not only presupposes a gift of the Spirit; it implies the active presence of his Person in the heart of the Christian . . . the love by which Christ has loved us and by which we, in our turn, can and must love our brethren, that is 'not only in word or speech but in deed and in truth' (1 Jn 3:18).

"The tree is judged by its fruits, and Saint Paul tells us that the 'fruit of the Spirit is love' (Gal 5:22) . . . .

"Be faithful to the directives of the great apostle. And, in accordance with the teaching of the same apostle, also be faithful to the frequent and worthy celebration of the eucharist (cf. 1 Cor 11:26-29). This is the way that the Lord has chosen in order that we may have his life in us (cf. Jn 6:53).

"In the same way, approach with confidence the sacrament of reconciliation. These sacraments express that grace comes to us from God, through the necessary mediation of the church.

"Beloved sons and daughters, with the help of the Lord, strong in the intercession of Mary, mother of the church, and in communion of faith, charity, and of the apostolate with your pastors, you will be sure of not deceiving yourselves. Thus you will contribute, for your part, to the renewal of the Church.

"Jesus is the Lord! Alleluia!"

Charismatics have received encouragement from the Holy Father. And in increasing numbers bishops are present at regional and international charismatic meetings. Such signs of encouragement by Church officials, however, do not entirely remove the curiosity, doubt, and even suspicion some Catholics harbor about charismatic manifestations. So, as an aid to understanding these gifts, the following descriptions are given of three charismatic gifts: *tongues, prophecy,* and *healing.* Each description also briefly indicates abuses of the gift, for often it is not the gift itself but certain dubious modes of behavior accompanying its exercise that onlookers find offensive.

The Gift of Tongues

Most often, though not always, the gift of tongues comes through the laying on of hands by other Christians who have already received this gift. Briefly described, praying in tongues means praising God either silently or vocally in unknown words, often expressed in melody.

A careful reading of the New Testament book, Acts of the Apostles, indicates that the gift of tongues played several different roles in the early Church. On the day of the first Pentecost, this gift enabled the apostles to communicate with Jews from many regions who otherwise would not have been able to understand the Gospel message (Acts 2).

But in most other passages where it appears in Acts of the Apostles, speaking in tongues appears to have been *in itself* a sign of the presence of the Holy Spirit, and in some cases the decisive sign (see, for example, Acts 10:44-48). Nonetheless, St. Paul says that interpretation is needed if this form of praise is to be truly beneficial to the whole community (1 Cor 14:1-5).

Passages in Acts about speaking in tongues meant nothing to me until I began to go to prayer meetings. Then I realized how the beautiful, haunting melodies combined with perfect harmony could be a sign of the Spirit. When one person prayed very loudly in tongues — and another brother or sister, given the gift of interpretation, loudly proclaimed the meaning of the foreign words — this combined manifestation seemed to be a message for the community.

In our age there is a constant hue and cry about lack of ability to communicate even in plain English. So isn't it amazing that some people would be gifted by the Spirit to understand words they never heard before?

A striking example I heard involved a man praying aloud in tongues, after which someone in the group gave an interpretation. After the meeting a Ukranian man excitedly announced that the language of the unknown tongue was a Ukranian dialect, and that the interpretation given by the interpreter — a person who had never heard that language — was absolutely accurate!

My own experiences of interpretation draw me very close to the inner core of the person praying in tongues. To think that I am "allowed" to participate in such a way in the inner life of another! It would seem to be almost irreverent did we not know from Scripture that this was part of the ordinary life of the early Church. Still we must confess that such experiences in the Spirit are a great mystery — a foretaste of heaven where no barriers of language will exist.

A typical contemporary prayer meeting includes much more than praying in tongues and the interpretation of special messages. There are readings from Scripture in English; there is teaching given by priests and other leaders that all those present may be encouraged to grow in love of God and neighbor. Everything points up the famous instructions of St. Paul on the primacy of love over all other gifts of the Spirit (1 Cor 13).

But, the skeptic may still wonder, why should praying in tongues be necessary for such growth in love? Books of Biblical theology mention this and other charisms as gifts needed by the early Church to impress the pagan multitudes. But why should such gifts suddenly appear in the 1970s?

From the standpoint of a lay person in the Church, I can see at least two main reasons why such a gift has meaning for our times.

The First Reason for These Gifts

The first reason for these gifts is the need for a sign of God's presence in our lives at a time when many Catholics are losing faith in that presence.

During the period immediately following Vatican II, increasing emphasis was placed on social concern. Catholics were urged to get out of their little "ghettos" of like-minded middle-class people and care about world problems. In the documents of Vatican II and in the social encyclicals of 20th-century popes, social justice was discussed in harmony with the supernatural aspects of the faith. But in much of the rhetoric following Vatican II, social justice was often stressed as if it was contrary to, and more important than, prayer and piety.

In the minds of many, doubt about St. Philomena was linked to skepticism about all miracles. There was a downgrading of Holy Scripture to the level of folk myths. Suspicion developed that belief in the unique truth of the Catholic Church was a form of intolerance, was unecumenical, was unchristian. This kind of popular theology was displayed on posters that said things like "Damn everything but the circus" and "My work is my prayer." In this type of atmosphere, it is not difficult to see why many sophisticated Catholics decided to do their best to be good people and let the supernatural alone. Since God was viewed more and more as the "ground of all being" and less and less as personal Savior, many lay Catholics gave up going to daily Mass and began to push prayer into the background.

In view of these factors I can see that there was a tremendous need for some new, unexpected sign of supernatural grace. The charismatic gifts, described in the New Testament, filled that need. They not only increased the faith of many in the presence of the Spirit today, but also counteracted the prevailing tendency to view Scripture as mainly symbolic and mythical. In these good effects, I see the first reason for the gift of tongues in our times. It is a light to those enveloped in the darkness of doubt.

The Second Reason for These Gifts

Then, too, the revival of charismatic gifts brought the warmth of the fire of the Spirit to many Catholics relatively untouched by the intellectual confusion of the day.

How many Catholics faithfully pray the rosary or some special devotion every single day of their lives and yet never seem to realize the personal love which Jesus has for them! When I think of my own daily prayers before the gift of tongues was released in me, I am amazed both at my perseverance and my coldness. I wonder now what Jesus was thinking as he saw me so faithful to prayer, yet so unwilling to listen or to drink in his love during that precious time together.

Though our motives in saying our daily

prayers faithfully may be very good, we may still fail to notice that there is something missing. We may attend an entire Mass or pray all five decades of the rosary without even caring that we have been completely distracted.

The choice for Christians is not between the dust and ashes of mechanical prayer and the forest fire of false mysticism. It is altogether possible, at least much of the time, that our prayer experience can be the growing warmth and light which come when we pray to Christ because we love and adore him and prepare ourselves to listen to his words of life.

There are many ways in which the Spirit may choose to reopen an individual of good will to a new experience of loving prayer. One of these ways is surely the gift of tongues. By means of this extraordinary grace the fire of the Spirit enkindles the spark of love for Christ. The felt assurance of his presence rewards the good intentions of those who have prayed faithfully for years.

It is claimed by some people that the most basic element of reality is sound. If there is a sense in which this is true, I theorize that each one of us has a unique sound at the core of our being — a sound which is released in the melody of our love song in the Spirit. This special love song which wells up from the soul in the melody of a strange tongue seems to me to be a reassurance of God's personal love. Such a theory would explain the remarkable sense of liberation from within which accompanies singing in tongues. It is a feeling that our deepest, usually hidden, spirit is flowing out toward God in the midst of the Body of Christ which is his Church. The childlike simplicity of being willing to pray in tongues publicly leads to more spontaneous praying in English in church or in the home.

In the liturgy Catholics recite aloud the beautiful words of the Psalms which are the very personal outcry of Old Testament saints. But many of these same Catholics consider it totally inappropriate to open their hearts to God in the same trusting, passionate way.

Due to long-existing custom, devotion outside of a ritual context makes many of us feel self-conscious about praying aloud. This, perhaps, is why some people accuse charismatics of ostentation and phoniness. Rather than shun personal public prayer, should we not pray fervently to the Holy Spirit to overcome this barrier of self-consciousness?

Abuses of the Gift of Tongues

Of course, there are abuses connected with the gift of tongues which seem to justify rejection of this charism. Let me try to explain how exaggerations of the gift arise.

Many persons, fresh from the experience of release through the gift of tongues, are amazed at the contrast between their previous mediocrity and their new-found fervent prayer in the Spirit. As a result, they run around telling everyone about it. Unfortunately, the impression often given is that all who do not pray in tongues are spiritually mediocre.

In their new-found enthusiasm such persons fail to recognize that, through Baptism and

Confirmation, *all* Catholics have received the gifts of the Spirit. A person who has never prayed in tongues may have a very deep interior love of Jesus and lead an exemplary life of service to others. Another person may pray the ritual words of the liturgy, wide-awake to their significance. The word of Scripture may be a source of deep union with Christ for others. Still others may pray the rosary with deep filial confidence and immersion in the mysteries — a practice by no means mechanical or drowsy.

Another abuse, one against which St. Paul admonished the Corinthians (1 Cor 13), is to revel in the delights of the Spirit to the detriment of sobriety and patient love. A person who questions the authenticity of these gifts is bound to be turned off even more if he sees a charismatic who has just praised God aloud for hours do a small unkind act. The onlooker may be judgmental in expecting perfection as a proof that the gifts are genuine. But the critic may be detecting a real danger: that the gifts can become an end in themselves, tempting us to neglect the duties of everyday life. No matter how supernatural praying in tongues may be in itself, it cannot substitute for the mundane task of caring for the needs of others, a task to which our Lord calls us moment by moment.

Prophecy

Most people identify the term *prophecy* with startling predictions about future events. The scriptural meaning of prophecy is much wider. In the Bible a prophet is one who transmits special words from God to the community. St.

Paul writes that "he who prophesies speaks to men for their upbuilding and encouragement and consolation" (1 Cor 14:3 — see also 2 Pt 1:20 and 1 Cor 12:10; 14:6, 26).

At a prayer meeting it is not uncommon for one of the participants to stand up and deliver a solemn message in the form of a first-person communication. "O my children, I love you. Do not fear for the future . . . ." Hearing such a prophecy for the first time can be quite startling. How can anyone dare to speak for God? Suppose it is not God?

During the seven years I have attended prayer meetings I have never heard a prophecy which was not in agreement with Scripture. But I have heard some prophecies which seemed more human than divine. And I can detect in my own self-examination what could be a temptation to abuse the gift in false prophecy. For example, sometimes when I am at a prayer meeting my mind is very busy thinking of how to refute a recent attack on God or the Catholic Church. On such occasions I wish that a voice from heaven would denounce the enemy in resounding, thunderous tones. I could easily phrase my thought in the first person, as if God was speaking, and say something like this: "O my children, do not walk among the scoffers . . . ." Perhaps if I got up and uttered such an admonition, some would believe that it came from God. Those who are more experienced, however, would probably detect a false human note in my voice and manner.

On the contrary, in valid instances of the gift of prophecy, the words begin as a voice in the heart, often unrelated to one's previous thought patterns. Often there is a sense that God wants me to speak those words even against my inclination to remain in the background. After the prophecy has been delivered, there is a feeling of completion, and often of trembling awe, as I drink in the meaning of the prophetic word for my life.

Importance of Prophecy for the Church

Why is the release of the gift of prophecy important for the contemporary Church? The following, I think, are several reasons.

Teachers of prayer sometimes ask their students to draw a diagram of their relationship with God. Many place God up at the top and put themselves as a speck at the bottom. Now on the basis of philosophy and theology we know that God, by the very nature of his being, must be *within* us as well as above us. Yet in the past, many Catholics tended to think of God *exclusively* as transcendent — that is to say, as so totally beyond us in every respect that he is infinitely distant from us. These Catholics thought of their prayers as something like telephone calls to outer space, and their spiritual life as a climb up an infinitely high mountain.

There is certainly truth in the concept of God as being infinitely beyond us. At the same time Jesus Christ is *the Word made flesh* dwelling among us. His presence is continued by means of the Eucharist. And he promised that "where two or three are gathered in my name, there am I *in the midst* of them" (Mt 18:20).

We all believe that Christ is with us. But when Catholics gather to pray, how seldom do we exhibit any expectancy that the living God will be among us, longing to set our hearts afire and to comfort us, as it were, under the wings of a dove? But in the words which come forth in prophecy, I see the Holy Spirit himself like a dove settling over our little group of Christians, gathering us to listen to his message of comfort or to hear his challenge to conversion.

Countless times I come to the prayer meeting in a state of fatigue or depression or anxiety about some problem I cannot handle on the human level. I imagine that nothing anyone could say will be able to help me. Then come words of prophecy giving the exact message I need at that moment to break through my despair.

Various Forms of This Gift

But many people still ask themselves: If this gift is so important, how could it have fallen into oblivion for so many centuries?

In the past few years I have read many lives of women saints in order to see the contrast between contemporary ideas of women's liberation and the true liberation that comes from closeness to God. In reading these accounts I have discovered that, although its expression often assumed other forms, the gift of prophecy was by no means dormant. The one most common form, in the lives of the saints and of many other persons who love the Lord, is hearing a word from God silently within one's heart. A common way of referring to such prophecies is to say, "It seemed to me that the Lord was telling me . . . ."

Of course, the release of the gift of prophecy depends partly on our human dispositions. I find that when I am very busy with my own projects or worries or obsessions, I tend to think of God as a means to my own ends — God is he who can make "x" happen. By contrast, I am most open to listen to God speaking to me when I have fallen into a pit and have to give up on my own efforts. At such times, however, I may be too distraught to hear the Spirit within my own heart. It is at such times that I am so grateful that his words can reach me at the prayer meeting through my brothers and sisters. Some of us have always pictured the contemplative gifts as taking place with God alone in total isolation from other human beings. It is a very humbling but beautiful revelation to find that God often chooses to come more deeply to one of his children through the ministry of others in the community.

Strange as it may seem, it is often in the midst of a huge crowd of charismatics, singing and clapping and praising God loudly, that the Spirit has led me to experience God's personal love for me in the depth of my soul. It is then that I seem to hear the Lord laughing gently at me and saying, "I never planned for you to make it alone. I love to draw my friends into union with one another through the hands of your brothers and sisters."

I think of the dovelike, comforting words of prophecy as being especially important also as an antidote to what might be called "gold-star spirituality." For years I imagined that God was like a grade-school teacher, giving me "gold stars" for each effort I would make. In spite of all the parables that Jesus tells us demonstrating the Father's merciful love for us, we can still fall into the "gold-star" mentality. Of course, the reason is our pride; we want to receive love as a merit badge rather than as a consolation prize! In reality it can be neither, for the love our God has for each one of us is a total, unmerited love, a love for a beloved one simply for what he or she is — the Lord's creation!

The words of prophecy ring out in the assembly, beginning with that humbling phrase, "O my children," and we are brought back to a true picture of ourselves. We are not glorious all-stars or despicable failures; we are weak but lovable children. Liable to fall down, always in need of the Father's comforting love, we are destined to grow and be strong in the strength of the Spirit.

Healing

Probably the most controversial of the charismatic gifts of the Spirit is *healing*. Most Catholics do believe in miracles. But miracles are thought to be few and far between, certainly not something to be counted on.

And yet it is impossible to read the story of Jesus and his early Church without coming across the theme of healing over and over again. To be a healer was simply one of the basic ministries of the early Church. "And God has appointed in the church first apostles, second prophets, third teachers, then workers of miracles, then *healers*, helpers, administrators, speakers in various kinds of tongues" (1 Cor 12:28).

On the subject of healing, the best treatment in the contemporary charismatic renewal is perhaps the book *Healing*, by Father Francis McNutt, O.P. (Notre Dame, Indiana: Ave Maria Press, 1974). This book is "must" reading for anyone interested in the gift of healing.

Here I would like simply to describe an attitude toward illness which I have experienced in myself and others, and show how the reality of healing in the Spirit helps to overcome such an attitude.

At times of physical and emotional illness, some of us tend to feel a certain shame; we try as much as possible to hide our pain behind a facade of superficial well-being. But when we are alone we drown in tears of self-pity, wondering what great wrong we have done to be so cruelly punished by God.

While we try to hide our real *anguish*, we are not embarrassed to discuss *details* of our illnesses with others. The part that can be treated as a neutral problem we enjoy discussing. But the part that cuts us to the quick, this we try to conceal. Doing so tends to make us bitter toward others and toward God.

In the Biblical accounts of healing, the sick person usually had to be willing to ask for help, or to be carried by friends to the feet of the healer. Many of us would find it very difficult to ask for healing, probably because we doubt if there is such a thing. And when we meet those who are suffering, we may want either to avert our gaze to avoid becoming depressed, or to empathize to the point of sinking under the burden of a shared despair.

What Can Be Done?

The question may be raised here: Is it true that we can do nothing for those who are suffering either physically or emotionally?

First of all, we can pray for those in pain. Catholics have always recognized the importance of prayer for the sick. But in charismatic praying, our concern is demonstrated outwardly by the laying on of hands and praying aloud, there and then, for the afflicted one. In doing this, we enfold the sufferer in our love as we entreat the healing presence of Jesus to bring about a cure.

Even when no visible healing seems to take place, the person in pain is helped. He or she experiences agony, not as an isolated personal stigma in a society of "beautiful people," but rather as an episode in the drama of his or her union with the crucified Savior. Jesus *could* remove all pain, but sometimes allows it for his own reasons of love.

Apart from physical healing, one of the most unique discoveries in the realm of charismatic healing is known as "healing of memories." Anyone who, in complete truth and sincerity, has experienced this process of healing under the direction of a Spirit-filled healer can never be quite the same person again! The best book on the subject I have found is by two priests, psychologists Dennis and Matthew Linn. The title is *Healing of Memories* (New York: Paulist

Press, 1975).

Many charismatic groups sponsor retreats or days of prayer centered on the gift of inner healing. At such times we are encouraged to open wounds of the past to the comforting love of Christ. And we are invited to forgive those who have hurt us. We begin to realize that these persons are not ogres, but people like ourselves. They are people who want to do good but who are weak, and have themselves been the victims of many wounds.

This is not to say that people experiencing severe emotional problems should not seek professional psychological help. But God can and does answer prayers for healing through the ministry of those trained to help.

We should always remember that Jesus himself wants to heal most of all our wounds of the heart: "Peace I leave with you; my peace I give to you; not as the world gives do I give to you. Let not your hearts be troubled, neither let them be afraid" (Jn 14:27).

Discernment and Other Gifts

As prayer groups grow in the Spirit, more and more of the gifts are released in response to needs which arise. I should like to indicate briefly some of these gifts.

As the Holy Father pointed out in his address quoted earlier, discernment is a gift of the greatest importance. By means of it the genuine works of the Spirit will be distinguished from those arising from purely human motives or from the lies of Satan (see 1 Cor 2:12-14; Phil 1:9).

Without such authoritative discernment, ultimately residing in Catholic groups in the voice of the pastor, the bishop, or the Pope as final authority, there is an ever-present danger of unbalanced but powerful leaders going off on a false tack and drawing people with them.

No matter how sincere, a leader may make wrong discernments because of his or her own peculiar psychological problems or intellectual confusion. Such a possibility always serves to increase my own deep awareness of what a gift we have in the Roman Catholic Church as the final source of judgment. Any group having difficulties of discernment can gain much from pondering the advice included in the Pope's address.

Wisdom and Knowledge

These gifts are needed for preaching and teaching, and also for discerning the truth about the way God is working in a particular situation. The most beautiful passage describing wisdom and knowledge as gifts of the Spirit is in chapter 1 of Ephesians. "I remember you in my prayers," writes St. Paul, "and ask the God of our Lord Jesus Christ, the glorious Father, to give you the Spirit, who will make you wise and reveal God to you, so that you will know him. I ask that your minds may be opened to see his light . . . . This power in us is the same as the mighty strength which he used when he raised Christ from death."

Administration and Helping

We rarely associate these terms used by St. Paul with charismatic prayer until we see them in operation. How refreshing to witness the swift, sure judgment of an administrator who is truly under the inspiration of the Spirit! How delightful to observe the quiet harmony of service which results when helpers are united in prayer in the Spirit!

On the other hand, some helpers and administrators fall away from guidance by the Spirit and develop a facade of amiability or prudence. Such a pseudo-affability can be a great obstacle to new people who come to visit a group. If the helpers greet newcomers with phony smiles instead of a genuine warm welcome, the people will go away discouaged and disillusioned. Administrators, too, who end all queries by pat statements of policy can have the same effect.

But when used sincerely under the direction of the Spirit, administration and helping can be channels of grace and power. As an example, I am thinking of an extraordinary woman who calls herself Jean "Books." She runs the book table at our prayer meetings and at many other meetings in the area. Because she has great gifts of wisdom and knowledge, she is able to discern real needs. Very often, individuals approach the table not seeking books but needing to talk to someone on an informal basis. Through prayer, Jean "Books" has learned how to determine which book would be most suitable in terms of the person's hidden need. Many times it is she who lays hands on someone in need of healing, who would be too shy to confess the problem before the larger group.

Praying for the Gifts

The most usual way of receiving the charismatic gifts of the Spirit is through a *Life in the Spirit Seminar.* At these seminars people dedicate themselves anew to Christ and open themselves in prayer to whatever gifts the Spirit may wish to release in them through the ministry of Spirit-filled Christians. But anyone can prepare for the gifts individually by ardent prayer and by being open to new life. An excellent book explaining how to have a Life in the Spirit Seminar in a Catholic parish is *You Will Receive Power,* by Sister Phillip Marie Burle, C.PP.S., and Sister Sharon Ann Plankenhorn, C.PP.S. (Pecos, New Mexico: Dove Press, 1977).

The following is a prayer written by the author for a Life in the Spirit Seminar given to a group of mothers.

Song of the Spirit

O mother, soothing a restless child upon
    your lap,
      You know he is asleep by certain sign —
        the softness of his breathing moves
        in rhythm with your own to the beat
          he learned
        so long ago within the womb, in his home
          beneath your heart.
    So shall we know that you, dear adult child
      of God,
        are deep in his great peace, by certain sign —
        in soft and rhythmic chant you murmur

lovely lullabies in strange but
friendly Spirit-tongues.
O father, you lift your babe aloft towards heaven
That he may see the whole world from on
high;
you let him ride atop your shoulders
that he may move onward with longer stride;
and then you bring him down to earth
again to show him how
to walk as big men do.
So would the Spirit raise you, grown-up
child of God,
to the heights of the divine,
to prophesy the vision of his glory,
the beauty of his great created world,
then plunge you deep into the well of
searing sacrifice
that you might know
the endless reach of selfless love
to which he beckons you.
Come Holy Spirit:
blow away the world-dust settling on
our homes,
give us singing hearts to praise the Lord,
bless our hands with gentle, healing touch,
root our minds in living faith and trust,
fire our lives that they may richly glow
in your unfathomed love.

A Life in the Spirit Seminar

4

The
Living Presence
of Christ
in the Sacraments

How deeply are those marvels of love, the holy sacraments of the Church, esteemed and appreciated by persons who have surrendered themselves completely to the Spirit!

Let me try to indicate, if only in a limited way, how personally each sacrament may be received and the abundance of sacramental grace that accompanies it when those participating in the ceremony are aware of and fully alive to the unique power contained in each sacrament.

(A very helpful book about the sacraments and renewal of parish life is *And Their Eyes Were Opened,* by Michael Scanlan and Anne Therese Shields [Ann Arbor: Servant Publications].)

Baptism

As all Catholics know, the Baptism of a baby or an adult marks the special, sacred moment of Christian initiation into the family of God.

The parents, godparents, other family members, and friends certainly would like to celebrate this event in the most beautiful way possible. Yet, how often the full impact of this first encounter with Christ is obscured by human elements accompanying the Baptism. There is the excitement of seeing the baby for the first time, admiration at the beauty of the baptismal robes, the distraction of watching expressions on the faces of those present.

Of course, the essential part of the sacrament, the special inpouring of grace on the one being baptized, is in no way affected by the attitudes of those in attendance. But liturgical piety calls for individual effort to pay attention to the leading of the Spirit in response to the holiness of the rite.

Accustomed to the vocal expression of praise, charismatics find it easier than most people to break through the barrier of conventional responses. They show their delight in word and action at the miracle of Christ's entering into full possession of his child whom he has called by name from all eternity. Rather than remaining satisfied with perfunctory, mumbling responses, charismatics enter into the spirit of the rite and participate in it fully.

The exorcisms are taken seriously as the rebuking of the Evil One who tempts us with lies about a happier life apart from the Lord. And often the sacred mystery of a Baptism offers the opportunity for a sincere renewal of baptismal vows by all present. "One thing have I asked of the Lord, that will I seek after; that I may dwell in the house of the Lord all the days of my life" (Ps 27:4).

Confirmation

In spite of herculean efforts on the part of religious educators, Confirmation is still misinterpreted and undervalued by many parents and teen-agers.

The gifts of the Spirit — wisdom, understanding, counsel, fortitude, knowledge, piety, and fear of the Lord — what value can they have for high school students who anticipate Confirmation time as little more than the beginning of their release from parental authority?

Often the parents of confused teen-agers are just as enmeshed as their children in a life style of compromise. Such parents do not dream of seeking the gift of fortitude to help them lead an apostolic life united with God. Much less do they think of making a commitment to seek moral perfection, or to pour out their lives in love of their neighbor. Their relationship to God resembles that which exists between an employee in a large company and the boss to whom he reports once a week. Such a situation is a far cry from the faithful sonship of a child of God who longs to dwell in the presence of his loving Lord.

Among the many different ways by which lukewarm Catholics can be awakened to the way of the Lord is the experience of the charismatic gifts.

During the Life in the Spirit Seminar — the preparation for Baptism in the Spirit — participants are asked to decide, for the first time or once again, whether they really want to follow the way of the Lord. Once a clear decision to live for Jesus has been made, the gifts of the Spirit bestowed at Confirmation are finally recognized for their inherent value. For the person strengthened in the Spirit, the gifts of wisdom, understanding, counsel, fortitude, knowledge, piety, and fear of the Lord come to be lived afresh as essential components of a Christian life style.

Centuries ago, St. Thomas Aquinas wrote that "everything is received according to the nature of the recipient." In relation to Confirmation, this means that a rebellious or fence-straddling recipient will experience little benefit from the gifts the Holy Spirit pours out in abundance.

As more and more children are brought up in Catholic homes in which the gifts of the Spirit are valued, the sacrament of Confirmation will come to be experienced as a real commitment to the Lord who loves each person with an individual love. The Lord longs to support teen-agers with his strength and his light as they struggle to find their own identity. He is their personal God who will lead them through trials in the comfort of his love and by the strength of the sevenfold gifts received in Confirmation. The love of his Spirit and the fire of his truth will rule their lives as they walk their pilgrim path to the Father.

Holy Communion

The Real Presence of Christ in the Eucharist is one of the sublime mysteries of our faith. In my little book entitled *Church of Love,* I try to show how Christ enters intimately into our very selves through this marvelous sign of his love.

Since the presence of his body and blood in the consecrated Host and in the cup is hidden from the eyes, Catholics have been taught through the centuries not to expect any special experience of him in the Eucharist. We are certainly not to seek after visions or ecstasies as the normal way of meeting Christ in the sacrament of Holy Communion.

In the early 1970s the attitude of many Catholics toward the Eucharist had become confused. Some approached the holy table in a mood of passive ritualism. Others, influenced by popular presentations of new theological concepts, began to doubt the need to believe in a real change of the substance of bread and wine into the body and blood of the Lord. Some catechetical texts written during this period tended to deemphasize the supernatural aspects of the Mass in favor of pointing out its value as the focus of human community.

As a result of this confusion, many young Catholics saw no reason to go to Mass at all. They could find many other ways to enjoy the company of their fellow human beings. And they could experience the God who is present everywhere just as well at the beach as in the chapel. As for older Catholics, there was a tendency among some to think of the Mass more as a symbolic, humanly satisfying ritual and less as a personal encounter with the Holy One who died for our sins.

In the midst of this tragic failure to respond to the sacredness of the Eucharist, it seemed to me as if the Spirit came down like a fire to rekindle the faith of Catholics in the Real Presence of the living Christ and to bring to naught all the pseudosophistication of false theologies. It was as if Jesus' words were coming true once again: "I thank thee, Father, Lord of heaven and earth, that thou hast hidden these things from the wise and understanding and revealed them to babes" (Mt 11:25).

What a joy it is to take part in liturgies in which faith in the Lord's Real Presence is manifested by priest and people alike. I am convinced that the thirst of the people for Christ will lead more and more to the rediscovery of him in the sacrament of the Eucharist.

Active participation by the People of God in

the Eucharistic Banquet is a dominant characteristic of the charismatic Mass. This encounter with the Real Presence of Christ takes the form of fervent outburst of praise and adoration followed by a hushed awe as he descends once again and becomes one with his children in a union of love.

The Sacrament of Reconciliation

The fire of the Holy Spirit reduces to ashes the wall we normally build around our chronic moral weaknesses. Phrases such as "Of course I always do this and that wrong thing, but I'm only human" cannot stand up to the challenge of the Holy Spirit in Scripture: "Be ye perfect as your heavenly Father is perfect." We have only to accept this astounding call to holiness and the Spirit will work miracles of change within us.

Whereas many Catholics of the 1960s and early 1970s had gotten into the habit of infrequent confession, it is no longer unusual to see long lines of Catholic charismatics waiting to be purified in the sacrament of Reconciliation. Often they have been brought to this point by the exhortations proclaimed in passages from Scripture during a prayer meeting.

Priests who hear confessions during prayer meetings tend to view the sacrament in terms of healing. They give their penitents time to express themselves and seek guidance at greater length than is normally possible. Even before the new rite was adopted, these priests had opened themselves to the gift of discernment so as to pinpoint the root of the penitent's trouble.

In sacramental Reconciliation one can observe bright, peaceful countenances as people emerge from the encounter with the forgiving Christ. By means of the understanding ministry of the priest the penitent, drawn under the wings of the dove, has discovered release in the Spirit and the new life that Christ came on earth to bring us.

I rejoice to think that in eternity all priests will know how many Catholics were saved by the love of Jesus transmitted to them through the fidelity of priests during long, hot hours in the confessional.

The new rite of Penance is ushering in a Church-wide renewal of the sacrament of Reconciliation — an awareness of it as an essential grace offered by our loving Savior for the forgiveness and rebirth of his people.

Marriage

Witnessing a marriage within a community of charismatics is an occasion when people who are suspicious have been most surprised and challenged.

The romantic beauty of the personal love of bride and groom is spotlighted in a marriage celebrated with charismatic prayer. But this unique love is centered on the heart of Christ. This is abundantly clear by the openness of all participants to his holy presence and by the fervent singing of hymns.

The group also shows its unity of heart through commitment to the couple. The marriage is viewed as a gift to the group. In exchange for this gift, the couple receives the abiding spiritual, psychological, and, if needed, economic support of the whole group.

I will never forget the first marriage I attended where the bride and groom were both charismatics. The groom was Steve Croskey, a leader in the Southern California Renewal. The bride was Melanie Dobies, a woman who had been associated with Steve in his work for many years. There was tremendous joy in the congregation, so many of whom had been ministered to by this pioneering couple in the charismatic renewal. Instead of the usual fidgety crowd, the whole group was united by a common bond of love in Christ, beautifully expressed in the stirring, fervent songs of the entire congregation. Father Ralph Tichenor, who had known the couple for years, presided at the ceremony. He now rejoiced with obvious delight in them and for them.

But there was another difference from most weddings — something everyone was aware of but of which no one had spoken: the bride was extremely ill. The marriage commitment of the couple to each other demanded a tremendous leap in faith, faith in a future which might never become a reality for them.

At the end of the service, the groom, breaking with tradition, made a startling announcement. "I composed a new song for this day," he said. "But I think there is an even better gift I can bestow on my bride. I am going to lay hands on her head, and I want you to join me in praying for her healing."

There was not a dry eye in the congregation as our voices united and ascended in deep intercessory prayer for our beloved Melanie. She *was* healed, through prayer and complicated surgery. And now, years later, when we see her healthy, radiant face and her little son in her arms, I doubt if there is any person who was present at that wedding who does not recall those moving moments of prayer.

At a time when marriage is one of the weakest bonds in society — promising much, but often bringing great disappointment — there is even more need than in prior centuries for Catholic couples to center their married lives in Christ.

Every good marriage and family demand a laying down of the lives of each for the sake of the others. And certainly, silent prayer for one another must bring down the blessings of God. But I find it even more Christian when the couple, freed in the Spirit, praise God and ask for his blessings in a visible, audible way.

I was touched to hear how one couple prayed aloud together during the birth of their first baby. How beautiful for the woman to have her husband praying with her during labor, and waiting to greet the baby with the words "Praise the Lord."

Aided by movements such as Marriage Encounter, couples are learning to communicate more openly with each other. But is it not just as important that couples pray over each other in times of trouble? How many tragic situations of estrangement begin with the feeling that "he or she doesn't care any more. Maybe God never wanted this marriage. Maybe it was all a mistake." Over and over again couples need to renew their vows. They need to call upon the graces of the sacrament of Matrimony and let the Holy Spirit pour refreshing waters of life-giving grace through the desert of boredom and taken-for-grantedness.

What a deep impression it makes on a child when every night father and mother place their hands on his or her little head in blessing! How comforting for a sick member to be prayed over by the family, warm wings of love surrounding the afflicted one. And how important for parents to pray for the inner healing of children at times of conflict.

Through the grace of the Holy Spirit many charismatic couples are inspired to celebrate the Sabbath with great joy and reverence — with singing, candles on the table, special prayers, and treats. As the ideal of Christian family life reemerges, old customs of celebrating feast days and special patron saints are being revived.

Holy Orders

One of the fruits of charismatic prayer (and of movements such as Marriage Encounter and Cursillo) is the renewal of love on the part of lay people for our priests.

The period after Vatican II, so fruitful and challenging in some ways, was also full of pain. Lay people became aware of the theological doubts of some admired clerical intellectuals. They were startled by the rage which began to show among priests and Sisters toward authority in the Church. And they were saddened by the growing exodus of vowed religious from their communities and commitments.

By the 1970s many Catholics who had

previously revered all priests came to regard some of them with suspicion. And in some schools, young people who had thoughts of a vocation to the religious life found priests and Sisters to be the ones who most discouraged them in their vocation.

Within the charismatic renewal, I find that the relationship between priests and lay people has a very unique flavor. It combines the best of the times before and after Vatican II. The holiness of the priestly vocation is understood again in terms of a call from Christ. It is seen as a call that is so strong that a man is willing to live a life of intimate union with Christ, which overflows in loving service to his people. Because charismatics are so in touch with the living presence of Jesus in the sacraments, they truly appreciate the uniqueness of the priest's mediating role.

There is also greater closeness than before between priest and people. The priest is seen not as an exalted figure, but as a brother in Christ whose own wounds need healing through the love of the community he serves. What a consoling sense of community strength in weakness, when a priest invites a group of lay people to place their hands on him and pray for his needs!

This new trust, built up in common prayer with the priest, opens us up in a new way to the priest's teaching authority. As a result, we can see more clearly how necessary it is to have true doctrine transmitted through the Holy Father, the bishops, and the pastors in their gifts of governance and teaching.

The Anointing of the Sick

During the disturbing period following Vatican II some Catholics began to think of Anointing of the Sick more as a mere ritual than as a holy means of healing grace. But the new attitude in the Church regarding the sacrament of anointing has changed all this.

We know that Jesus wants to comfort and heal us. As the Spirit descends like a dove in the anointing of our sick bodies, a cessation of fear and anxiety is experienced. This is the power of Jesus coming to us just as certainly as when he laid hands on the sick during his life on earth. Having seen extraordinary healings accompanying the sacrament of anointing, I have become much more aware of the presence and power of Jesus.

But what of the troubled questions that arise: "Suppose I am not healed? Does he love others more, since he healed them and not me? Is my own lack of faith the reason?"

Mystery of his love! There is no mathematical answer to prayer. In the reassurance of his presence we can say with Job, "The Lord gave, and the Lord has taken away; blessed be the name of the Lord!" (Jb 1:21) No matter how much we want to live on to serve God, or how much we are overwhelmed by the natural fear of death, our greatest wish as Christians must simply be to accept the will of God.

In the movie *The Hiding Place*, based on the book by Corrie Ten Boom, two sisters are persecuted by the Nazis for hiding Jews. I was deeply impressed by the faith of the one sister who was tortured the most. In answer to the question, "Why would God let you, who are so good, suffer so much?" she replied: "If you *know him,* you don't have to know why."

What a tremendous grace of the Holy Spirit to be able to say we truly know Jesus and his love for us; that we do not have to fear death as the worst evil; that our whole life has one purpose: to grow in love of God and neighbor. In time of serious illness when dread and fear tend to drive us toward despair, we welcome the pure presence of Jesus in his sacrament of anointing. We know that he can either heal us or draw us closer to himself while he walks with us through the valley of the shadow to our eternal home.

Mary, Bride of the Spirit

5

Mary,
Our Model,
Bride
of the Spirit

Our Lady of the Annunciation,
  pure of heart
    swift to discern
    pondering the Word . . .
  Announced by an angel,
    the Spirit overshadowed you like a dove;
    no smog of evil impeded his entrance,
      "Behold the handmaid of the Lord,
      be it done to me according to your
        will."
  Unloose our tense fingers . . .
    that we with open hands
    may receive the Lord as Gift.

Our Lady of the Visitation,
  thoughtful heart . . .
    leaping over the mountains
    quietly pondering your unique destiny,
  aflame with prophetic utterance:
    "My soul magnifies the Lord,
    and my spirit rejoices in God my Savior,
    for he has regarded the low estate of
      his handmaiden.
    For behold, henceforth all generations
      will call me blessed;
    for he who is mighty has done great
      things for me."
  Kindle in us a spirit of grateful joy,
    prophesy our unique calling,
    stir our hearts to sacrificial love,
    a love that brooks no obstacle.

Our Lady of the Nativity,
  before time was born . . .
    chosen among God's privileged ones
    to give to sinful man a God-Man-Savior.

In tender, grateful awe you contemplate your
Son,
and join in jubilant song of praise:
"Glory to God in the highest,
and on earth peace among men with
whom he is pleased!"
Give us the grace of still wonder,
teach us to hold and cherish his Mystery,
to contemplate the Word made flesh
concealed in all created things.

Our Lady of the Presentation,
Bride of the Spirit,
carrying your child in your arms —
your God,
to offer him in his own house
to our Father.
You did not flinch from the sword of
sorrow
as you prayed that all God's pilgrim
people
might see the
"light for revelation to the Gentiles,
and for glory to thy people Israel."
"And a sword will pierce through
your soul also,
that thoughts out of many hearts may
be revealed."
Heal with the ointment of praise
lips chapped and charred by the stale,
harsh
words of the world.
Strengthen the heavy-laden with the milk
and honey of your Good News.

Our Lady of the Hidden Years,
  pure sister of God's children,
    walking compassionately with the poor,
      ever ready to serve, unheeding of cost,
      filling the hungry with tidings of joy,
      "keeping all these things in your heart."
  Nurture in us the fruits of the Spirit,
    that we may love in deed and in truth,
    serve with joy, patience, peace, kindness,
    goodness, self-control, forgiveness
    in faithful dedication.

Our Lady of the Cross,
  valiant mother, wrapped in anguished grief,
    reflecting every quiver of your Son's pain
      that grace might flow through you
      in boundless measure
      to all your children who
        "groan inwardly as we wait for the
        adoption as sons . . .
        the Spirit himself interceding for us
        with sighs too deep for words."
  Do not abandon us
    when pain overwhelms,
      as we agonize for our sins . . .
    when dark despair would clutch at our
      hearts
      and we suffer at the hands of those we
        love,
    teach us our part in the saving mission of
      the world.

Our Lady of Pentecost,
  Mother of the Church born in the Upper
    Room,

The sons and daughters of the promise
"devoted to prayer . . .
with Mary the Mother of Jesus,"
came forth afire with the gifts of the
Spirit
to build up his Church . . .
to unite all in One.
Draw all men into his presence
that his Church may be renewed in the
Spirit,
and his people go forth to radiate
the fire of truth . . .
the comfort of the dove
to the dark, cold, beautiful world
he came to save.

Our Lady of the Assumption,
beauty ineffable,
borne in the fire of the Spirit
on the wings of the dove
from time to eternity,
queened and clothed in the radiance of
your Son.
Ever mindful of your earthly children,
you come to them in wondrous
apparitions.

O Virgin, Bride of the Spirit,
fill us with untold inner joy
that we may shun all shades of sin.

O Mother,
symbol of the abiding love of our God,
hold us close in your Sacred Heart
and still our fears.

O Sister,
>   be with us when we pass through the
>   valley of the shadow.
>   Lead us to the throne of your
>   divine Son, our Brother — our God.

Hail Mary, full of grace, the Lord is with
you,
>   blessed are you among women and
>   blessed
>   is the fruit of your womb, Jesus.

Holy Mary, Mother of God,
>   pray for us sinners
>   now and at the hour of our death.

> *Amen. Alleluia!*

Father Ralph Tichenor, S.J.

(6)

An Interview
with Father
Ralph Tichenor, S.J.

This is a book of personal reflections, the witness of a lay participant in the charismatic renewal. It seems advisable, therefore, to conclude this book with answers to some controversial questions — answers that come from a more authoritative source. With this object in view I requested an interview with Father Ralph Tichenor, S.J. — priest, scholar, and one of the most experienced leaders in the charismatic renewal. Father Tichenor is President of Southern California Renewal Communities, an organization which ministers to more than 225 prayer groups in the Los Angeles area.

CHERVIN: *Father, in your opinion, what is the most essential feature that makes a person a charismatic?*

FATHER TICHENOR: A charismatic is one who has received and uses a new experience in the Holy Spirit. Such a person is generally found to have a deep love for Scripture. Since the Paraclete was sent to teach us all things that Christ taught, it would be strange if people who have received the Spirit are not experiencing a newness of relationship with the Lord, a relationship characterized by the use of the Scriptures. I believe this is the most essential sign. It is interesting to note that when people talk about losing the charisms, they have generally ceased to read Scripture.

CHERVIN: *Would you say, then, that the gift of tongues is not an essential mark of charismatic prayer?*

TICHENOR: Some non-Catholic groups who do

not have a sacramental understanding of the Church use the gift of tongues as a visible sign of unity with the Spirit. Catholics, however, believe that the Spirit comes through the sacraments, especially Baptism.

On the other hand, I do believe that the Holy Spirit is pouring out the charismatic gifts — including the gift of tongues — on all Catholics just as during the infancy of the Church. When St. Paul wrote that tongues was considered the least of the gifts, I think the reason was that it was the gift common to all Christians.

CHERVIN: *Rather than a question of a special grace of God given only to a few, would you say then that the barrier to praying in tongues is always on the part of the recipient?*

TICHENOR: Yes. And there can be many reasons. A person may not understand the gift and therefore not be open to it; others may fear turning themselves over to the Lord.

An interesting thing I have observed is that language teachers have a special difficulty with tongues. They are used to thinking of language in terms of rules and therefore find spontaneous praying in an untaught, unstructured language a difficulty.

Those who do not pray in tongues, for whatever reason, should pray for the gift until they receive it, for this very valuable grace will increase the depth of their freedom in praying to the Lord.

CHERVIN: *In his May 1975 address to the International Conference of Charismatics (quoted earlier), the Holy Father, Pope Paul VI, emphasized the importance of proper guidance of charismatic groups by ordained priests. Is such guidance really in action? Should every prayer group be led by a priest?*

TICHENOR: In all enthusiastic movements there is a danger that enthusiasm will carry people beyond the Scriptures and what the Church teaches. As a result, it is almost essential that there be careful guidance of the larger prayer groups and a care for the smaller ones. The natural person to turn to is the priest whose theological training should give him an understanding of the dangers. In some cases, however, a layman with theological training or a religious might substitute for the priest.

In any case, since the sacramental aspect is just as important as the charismatic aspect, a priest is always needed to complete the renewal of the Church.

In other words, while not absolutely necessary as a participant in every prayer meeting, a priest is most important as a guide. Almost all the problems arising in prayer groups come from a lack of theological care on the part of the priest. The lay people in any group should actively seek the guidance of the priest.

CHERVIN: *What if the priest in a given parish does not approve of charismatic prayer and therefore rejects the group?*

TICHENOR: A priest really has no right to reject a spiritual movement unless it has been rejected by the hierarchy of the Church or the Pope. The charismatic renewal has not been rejected and in many cases has been encouraged. Whatever a priest's personal attitude may be, he is a shepherd of the entire flock. Therefore he has to accept responsibility for any group within the parish, whether they meet in the church or in a private home. He does not necessarily need to be an active participant in the group, but he should give them guidance.

If, because the priest does not wish a group to use Church facilities, they meet in a private home and their number increases beyond the accommodations, they may appeal to the priest and the bishop for a larger space.

CHERVIN: *What is the relation between the charismatic gifts and the sacraments? For example, is the so-called baptism of the Holy Spirit a duplicate of Confirmation? Or are healing prayers a substitute for the sacrament of the Anointing of the Sick?*

TICHENOR: The sacraments give us the gifts through the Spirit, but they are not the same as the charismatic gifts. The gift of healing is given in all the sacraments, particularly the sacrament of Reconciliation and the Eucharist. The Anointing of the Sick should be administered when there is serious illness. The charismatic gift of healing is operative both as part of the sacraments, but also as separate from the reception of the sacraments. In general, the gift of healing is given to those who have already received the sacraments, especially Baptism.

For years the Church emphasized the sacraments to such an extent that many people lost sight of the charismatic gifts. Now there is a danger of the reverse. Some experience the

Spirit so beautifully in charismatic prayer that they feel no need for the sacraments. The Church existed, although not so freely as it should have, without emphasis on the charisms; but it could never exist with the charisms only and not the sacraments.

True unity in the Church comes through the sacraments, and the Eucharist is the source of that unity. Though our gifts are different, we are one because we all receive one Lord and our unity is enhanced by the outpouring of special graces.

Therefore, a Catholic cannot become a better Christian by rejecting the sacraments in favor of the charisms. On the contrary, his charismatic gifts will strengthen his love and appreciation of the sacraments, the channels of God's special grace to his people.

CHERVIN: *How do you explain the fact, then, that so few people experience the gifts of the Spirit in Confirmation, while so many, when prayed over by charismatics for the release of the Spirit, do experience them (baptism of the Spirit)?*

TICHENOR: Confirmation is a sacrament, and the sacrament is truly received even if there is no experience of change. Baptism of the Spirit is not a sacrament; it is an experience. To have the full benefit of the sacrament one should expect to receive the charismatic gifts in a new way. But many have not experienced them because of lack of expectation. Now that Catholics have a better understanding of the charismatic gifts, it is probable that the reception of the sacrament of Confirmation will be accompanied by a greater visible outpouring of graces.

CHERVIN: *Does charismatic prayer tempt some Catholics who have difficulties with the Church to leave the Church and join interdenominational groups?*

TICHENOR: Unfortunately, it sometimes happens that the emotional fervor of charismatic prayer makes the usual worship in the Church seem too intellectual by contrast. There is little doubt that the Church has been far too intellectual in its approach of late. One of the reasons why many priests and religious find difficulties with the charismatic renewal is that they have difficulty with their own emotions. The combination of the intellect and the emotional leads to maturity and fullness in the Christian. Rather than retarding the renewal which is truly the way the Spirit is working in the Church, this problem should lead her (the Church) to encourage the charismatic renewal in the parishes.

CHERVIN: *Because of its original links with Protestant theology, does charismatic prayer lead to an underplaying of Catholic traditions in favor of fundamentalist approaches?*

TICHENOR: It could. But on the contrary, charismatic prayer should lead us to learn from the fundamentalists the beauty of their way of praying to the Lord. It should encourage us to have more freedom of emotion, not only in our private prayer but also in our liturgies — since it is through our emotions that we express our deepest convictions.

Of course, emotions should be real and honest — without affectation, and manifested in a way which is not disturbing to liturgical order. Isn't a new spirit of released joy one of the elements most needed today in our parishes?

The fundamentalists can also teach us a real love of the truth of Scripture.

CHERVIN: *Does charismatic piety tend to become an end in itself with a consequent lack of concern for social issues?*

TICHENOR: The basic concern of the charismatic experience of the Spirit is love and love is not a word. It is a deed. The charismatic who is satisfied with prayer and no action is not truly following the Spirit.

The social apostolate based on the love of God and of neighbor is essential to a complete charismatic renewal. Many great men and women have lost their Christian heritage by forgetting that prayer must be the basis of all our actions for God. Now the charismatic renewal is a prayer movement, so there is less danger of a charismatic making the social apostolate more important than the prayer-based work of the Church. But the danger of stopping with prayer is real and at times has manifested itself. This is a rejection of the Spirit.

There are many prayer groups at this time who have taken up some particular work of social action such as running orphanages, building schools, visiting the sick, sharing food with the poor. It is expected that as a prayer group matures it will find similar tasks.

CHERVIN: *Regarding the inner life of the prayer group, there are many questions which are frequently asked. Here are two of them: Are prayer groups divisive of families? Should a husband or a wife participate if the spouse is unfavorable to the idea?*

TICHENOR: If tensions which cannot be handled through dialogue arise in a marriage because of participation by one of the partners in prayer meetings, the sacrament of Matrimony demands accepting the limitations of the spouse and acceding to his or her desires. It is the general policy of prayer groups to discourage participation when the partner in the marriage objects. The Spirit creates unity, not disunity.

CHERVIN: *What is the role of women in the charismatic renewal? Is it true that they are discouraged from leadership positions?*

TICHENOR: There is no doubt that there has been and there still is a real emphasizing of male domination in the renewal. The usual appeal to St. Paul without taking into account the many women — Lydia, Priscilla, and so on — who were instrumental in building the Church with Paul, is a mistaken one. We are learning from our mistakes. Leadership should be given by the Holy Spirit and discerned by the community. If the Spirit gives the gift of leadership to a woman, the community has no right to reject her gift.

CHERVIN: *Many people have difficulty with the way in which prophecies are phrased. It seems presumptuous when a person gets up and speaks for God in the first person. For example: "Oh my children, I want you to know that. . . ." Wouldn't it be more in keeping if the prophet said, "It seems to me that the Holy Spirit wants me to convey this message"?*

TICHENOR: The person should give a prophecy as the Lord gives it to him or her. If God puts it in the first person, we should not show doubt by using such terms as "seems"; we should speak out boldly the word of the Lord. If we are not sure, then of course it is necessary to guard people from error by expressing our lack of secure judgment.

A group may get into a habit of introducing prophecy in a certain manner such as "My little children." But the real prophecy is the content. If I hear the Lord saying to prophesy, I have to prophesy in his name.

Discernment of prophecy is based on how people experience that prophecy as directed to them. In this case they should respond vocally so that the prophet gets a confirmation of the message. To respond automatically with "Praise the Lord" is confusing to the prophet and to the leaders.

CHERVIN: *Is witnessing somewhat exhibitionistic?*

TICHENOR: Yes. A good preacher is a good actor. One who wishes to arouse people to action must be dramatic in some way. Most evangelizing or witnessing has an exhibitionist aspect.

When exhibitionism attracts attention to the individual rather than to the message, then it is wrong and self-defeating. One who is witnessing should really concentrate on the message, in which case it will draw people not to the person himself but to the Lord.

CHERVIN: *What about healing services? Some observers think that charismatics demanding instant healings, consolations, and so forth fail to appreciate the role of the cross in the life of every Christian. This problem seems particularly acute in the case of people who are brought to healing services with high expectations which fail to materialize. Then they think they lack faith, which adds to their miseries. Wouldn't it be better to preach the cross instead of raising false hopes?*

TICHENOR: There are several important aspects to this question. In their joy at the experience of the Spirit, a great number of charismatics forget the way of the cross for a time. It often comes to them as a shock that they have not been freed from the burdens of life. They may pass through a time of rejecting trials as coming from evil spirits and not from ordinary relationship problems that even holy people experience, or from the vicissitudes of the culture, or from nature itself. This is a phase which must be overcome, for the way of the cross is the way of all true Christians who follow the Master.

With regard to healing services, there are many false ways of formulating the expectation of healing. First of all, God does not heal us because we have faith. Nor is healing a reward for our merits. God can heal even when there is no faith present. Faith is an ordinary vehicle, but the basic condition for a healing is not so much faith as total forgiveness of oneself and others. To be a Christian you must love, and to love you must forgive.

Some people are not healed because God desires to deepen their spirituality or to strengthen their virtues or those of others.

At the same time, we must see that on earth Christ always showed a dislike for sickness and often healed people. We should not reject a healing offered to us because of false humility or lack of trust in the divine mercy.

God answers healing prayers in unexpected ways. For example, he may heal someone in a wheelchair not of the crippling, but of emotional difficulties. God does not always give us the gift we ask for, but what we would ask for if we knew better. We see everything on a vertical line but God sees it as a point.

For these and other reasons, it is wrong and very unloving for anyone — unless he has a special prophetic gift of knowledge of healings — to proclaim at a healing service that someone would be healed if "he had more faith."

CHERVIN: *What is prophetic healing?*

TICHENOR: It is the knowledge of God's desire to heal a particular person from a particular illness. Sometimes the person with the gift of prophetic healing can see the illness even when the afflicted one does not know he has that particular illness.

CHERVIN: *Do you think some of the healings are more psychological than physical?*

TICHENOR: Katherine Kuhlmann said that 80 percent of the healings are psychological, but she pointed out that it is the psychosomatic illnesses which are the most difficult for doctors to heal! Healing should be seen in the context of new life: new ability to love and reach out; forgiveness which helps not only the one who forgives but also the forgiven one who was formerly bound. A person who is unwilling to forgive harms not only himself but the other person as well.

CHERVIN: *So what should be the attitude of a person going to a healing service? Should he expect to be healed or not?*

TICHENOR: He should come with an openness to the will of God and expect that God will do those things any loving person would do — that is, what is best for the one he or she loves.

CHERVIN: *Speaking of the psychological, some people see loud praise "orchestrated from the platform" as a manifestation of mass psychology rather than the work of the Holy Spirit. What do you think?*

TICHENOR: I agree with Father Richard Rohr, warning against the "domestication" of the Holy Spirit through domination of leaders who, consciously or unconsciously, may try to determine what the Spirit should be doing rather than what the Spirit wants to do. This makes for artificiality at assemblies and would even be hypocritical if it were deliberate.

In charity we must not make the judgment that a manifestation of praise is hypocritical or artificial, but we must make the judgment whether it is genuine guidance of the Spirit at work. The community must discern whether the leader is guiding the meeting in an appropriate manner or whether he is honestly mistaken and unconsciously imposing his or her own personality on the group.

CHERVIN: *What is the theological significance of slaying in the Spirit? (Individuals at prayer meetings seem to faint on coming into contact with a very charismatic leader.) Many people think that such phenomena are oversensational and give too much power to the minister. If it is valid, under what circumstances is it good?*

TICHENOR: "Resting in the Spirit" is a better phrase. The basis for it is rather weak, although there are texts in both the Old and New Testaments which indicate that resting in the Spirit by individuals and groups does sometimes take place. The obvious example is at the dedication of the Temple when the priests were overcome by the cloud and could not enter into the Temple (1 Kgs 8:10-13; 2 Chr 5; Dn 8:17-18). There is also a passage in Revelation (1:10-20, especially verse 17).

It is obvious that the outpouring of the graces of the Spirit, especially when unexpected, can overpower an individual. Therefore, it is not surprising that this should take place. Many people feel that the genuine experience of resting in the Spirit leads to a maturing of graces and to a deepening relationship with the Holy Spirit.

It is an abuse when people feel they should have this experience as a badge — or if the minister, for the sake of vainglory, hopes that people will be slain in the Spirit as the result of his ministry. But just because there can be imperfect emotions connected with it, we should not reject this way of receiving the Spirit and his gifts.

A minister should never try to control the situation. Nor should he impose psychological attitudes which arouse expectancy of being slain in the Spirit. This experience should be understood as an overflow of grace. As with all other gifts, we should seek not the gift for its own sake but the Giver himself.

CHERVIN: *Another extremely controversial matter involves the idea of "headship" — submission of a member of a prayer group to the spiritual direction of a leader. Do you think that leaders have sufficient theological training to impose such submission?*

TICHENOR: With regard to Catholic communities or Catholics in ecumenical communities, the term "headship" has been associated with a leadership which claims that authority comes directly to it. This sounds and often is authoritarian. Many religious orders recognize in this practice problems which they experienced with this kind of leadership before Vatican II.

The true head of a charismatic prayer community is the Holy Spirit. Those who are chosen to guide the group are and should always act as servants. Their main source of guidance comes from prayer, discernment, and loving concern of the community for good order. Such leadership can be dangerous if the head does not know

Catholic doctrine or is not completely open to the Spirit who guides him (more often through the Church than directly).

It is a heresy to think that a group is being guided always by direct inspiration of the Spirit without regard to Scripture, tradition, dogma, and the authority of the hierarchy.

The head should never assume to himself the gifts of ordination unless he is in fact an ordained minister. The community members are bound by their sacramental gifts to resist any usurpation of the powers of the ordained clergy or of the hierarchy.

CHERVIN: *Do all covenant communities (groups taking a vow to support each other in all ways under the headship of a leader) have the approval of the bishop?*

TICHENOR: All communities should seek legitimacy through the hierarchy.

CHERVIN: *Thank you very much, Father, for your very illuminating answers. In summary, how would you describe the ideal prayer group?*

TICHENOR: A group of Christians dedicated to prayer, sharing the Spirit, praising the Lord, and living in love with their neighbors.

Notes

Notes

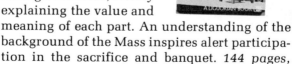

Other books
by Ronda Chervin

The Spirit and Your Everyday Life

You can fill your everyday actions and conversation with faith, hope, and love if you call on the graces of the Holy Spirit to help you. *64 page booklet, $1.00.*

Prayer and Your Everyday Life

Helps you develop a personal relationship with God. The author shows where God fits into your daily routine and how you can yield your life to him. *64 page booklet, $1.00.*

Love and Your Everyday Life

Helps you strive for perfect love of God in everyday life. Dr. Chervin explains how the Holy Spirit can help you deal with imperfections (yours and others). *64 page booklet, $1.00.*

* Includes prayer exercises
and Scripture quotes.

◀ To Order

THE **LIGUORIAN** MAGAZINE

published monthly by the Redemptorists

If you want to know what's going on in
  the Catholic Church today,
    look to the LIGUORIAN.

If you want guidance in some of today's
  moral dilemmas,
    look to the LIGUORIAN.

If you want ideas mixed with ideals,
    look to the LIGUORIAN.

And if you just want a good
all-round magazine that offers
information, inspiration, and motivation —
with stories, cartoons, a special feature for
the youngsters, a special "under 21" feature
for teens, special interest articles for singles,
married couples, and senior citizens,
    look to the LIGUORIAN.

5 years @ $15.00
3 years @ $10.00
1 year @ $5.00
(Add $1.00 per year outside U.S.A.)

Send your name and address to:
The **Liguorian**
One Liguori Drive, Liguori, Mo. 63057

20
26

Come, Holy Spirit, enkindle in us the fire of your love!

The fire and the dove, the gifts of the Spirit, the third Person of the Trinity . . . all of these have long been a familiar part of Catholic prayers and devotions. But today they have taken on new life, depth, and meaning in the charismatic movement.

In this book, popular author Ronda Chervin speaks candidly on such misunderstood topics as prophecy, healing, and the gift of tongues.

Drawing from her own personal experience, Dr. Chervin explains the charismatic gifts of the Spirit. She then briefly outlines how each of the Church's sacraments can be experienced more fully by those who have surrendered themselves to the Spirit. The author concludes the book with an enlightening interview of charismatic leader Father Ralph Tichenor, S.J., President of Southern California Renewal Communities.

This is a book for anyone who wonders about the charismatics. This is a book for those who are charismatics. This is a book charismatics can give to those who question them about their devotion to the Holy Spirit.

This is a book that offers understanding through the fire of faith and the peace of God's love.

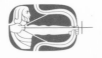

Liguori Publications
One Liguori Drive
Liguori, Mo. 63057
(314) 464-2500

KQ-025-065